RETHINKING
ACTOR'S BODY

RETHINKING THE ACTOR'S BODY

Dialogues with Neuroscience

Dick McCaw

methuen | drama

LONDON · NEW YORK · OXFORD · NEW DELHI · SYDNEY

METHUEN DRAMA
Bloomsbury Publishing Plc
50 Bedford Square, London, WC1B 3DP, UK
1385 Broadway, New York, NY 10018, USA

BLOOMSBURY, METHUEN DRAMA and the Methuen Drama logo
are trademarks of Bloomsbury Publishing Plc

First published in Great Britain 2020

Cover design by Charlotte Daniels
Cover image: Diagram of the nervous system (sixteenth century) by
Andreas Vesalius (© Bridgeman Images)

A catalogue record for this book is available from the British Library.

Names: McCaw, Dick, author.
Title: Rethinking the actor's body : dialogues with neuroscience / Dick McCaw.
Description: London ; New York : Methuen Drama, 2020. | Includes bibliographical
references and index. | Summary: "How does an actor embody a character? How do
they use their body as an instrument of expression? Rethinking the Actor's Body offers
an accessible introduction to the fields of neurophysiology and embodied knowledge
through a detailed examination of what an actor does with their body. Built on almost
a decade of conversations and public seminars by the author Dick McCaw in partnership
with John Rothwell (Professor of Neurophysiology at University College London, UK),
Rethinking the Actor's Body explores a set of questions and preoccupations concerning
the actor's body and examines overlaps in research and practice in the fields of actor
training, embodied knowledge and neurophysiology"– Provided by publisher.
Identifiers: LCCN 2019043889 | ISBN 9781350046467 (hardback) | ISBN
9781350046474 (paperback) | ISBN 9781350046450 (pdf) | ISBN 9781350046481
(epub) | ISBN 9781350046498
Subjects: LCSH: Movement (Acting)–Psychological aspects. | Acting–Psychological
aspects. | Actors–Psychology. | Cognitive neuroscience. | Neurophysiology. | Neurosciences
and the arts.
Classification: LCC PN2071.M6 M386 2020 | DDC 792.02/8–dc23
LC record available at https://lccn.loc.gov/2019043889

ISBN: HB: 978-1-3500-4646-7
          PB: 978-1-3500-4647-4
        ePDF: 978-1-3500-4645-0
       eBook: 978-1-3500-4648-1

Typeset by Integra Software Services Pvt. Ltd.
Printed and bound in Great Britain

To find out more about our authors and books visit www.bloomsbury.com
and sign up for our newsletters.

To Jonathan Grieve
How many hours have we spent talking about
theatre, performance and training?

CONTENTS

PART TWO

8 The Emotional Body 193

9 Bringing It All Back Home 223

FIGURES

PREFACE

Rethinking the Actor's Body: Dialogues with Neuroscience is the companion volume to *Training the Actor's Body: A Guide* which was published in 2018. In 2014 I was commissioned to write a book on actor training which I provisionally called *The Actor's Body: A Guide*. I had in mind a book that resembled the Haynes Manuals which used to offer detailed mechanical guides for some 300 models of motor cars and motor bikes. These were for DIY enthusiasts who were fascinated by what happens under the bonnet of their car.

Composition

Having just published my book *Bakhtin and Theatre* in January 2016, I began work on *The Actor's Body*. By June I had written some 60,000 words which turned out to be mostly theoretical questions concerning the actor's body. My patient editor, John O'Donovan, pointed out that this clearly was not the practical book on actor training that he had commissioned. He suggested that I begin work on the practical book and make a proposal for my more theoretical book. The typescript of my theoretical chapters was then sent for review to two readers and was also read by my friend (and Bakhtin expert) Caryl Emerson. Their comments and suggestions have been hugely helpful, and have resulted in a complete restructuring of this book. A reader may well ask about the relation between the two books and which one should be read first? Certainly, *Rethinking the Actor's Body* is no longer an introduction to *Training the Actor's Body*. I am equally sure that both books stand alone as studies even though there are many connections between them. Maybe they are one rather long book about the actor's body?

Now a word about the content of this book. I have been reading books about neuroscience for some twenty or so years now, but what first compelled me to try and integrate my scientific reading and my practical work into a sustained study was a question that I experienced in class. I was watching my students work and while most of them were simply messing about, two were playing some kind of game. One student was standing behind the other, holding her by the waist. The student behind then started carefully kicking behind the knees of the one in front causing her legs to swing forward. A few things about this game were clear: it was fun, it was clearly an experiment even if they didn't know where it might lead and it demanded all their attention. This was a kind attentive play that might or might not generate material that they could then develop into a performance. Although I instinctively knew the difference between the horseplay of most of the class and the heuristic play of these two students, I also knew that beneath this observation there lay other more fundamental questions about the mental and emotional state of actors at work. This problem concerning the connection between attention, play, and conscious and unconscious work prompted me to write what can only be called a proto-book called *Between Body and Brain* in 2008.

Between Body and Brain turned out to be little more than an attempt to try and make sense of all the books on neuroscience that I had read up to that point. From these pages I drew an article called 'Plumbing or Wiring?' (2009). The title was a provocation based on two very different models by which the actor's body can be understood: the first is a 'hydraulic' notion of how the human body is animated by energy which courses like a liquid through channels, the second being the complex 'wiring' of the brain and its nervous systems by means of which the body moves and feels. The present book returns to these two very different approaches to understanding the human body in action. Underlying each approach is a very different way of understanding and knowing. Actor training is a ruthlessly pragmatic approach which draws on a vast range of unacknowledged sources of knowledge which consist variously of lore, of 'common sense' and of written sources (books by actors and actor trainers). Neurophysiology couldn't be more different and concerns the scientific research into the nervous system and the different parts of the brain. The present book is an attempt to tie my reading of the neuroscientific literature more closely with problems of actor training (many of which have been addressed in *Training the Actor's Body*).

There are strong connections in the approach of this book and that of my earlier book, *Bakhtin and Theatre* (2016) where I set up a dialogue between two different kinds of knowledge which were tested against each other. On one side there were the theoretical writings of Mikhail Bakhtin and on the other the writings and transcripts of Stanislavsky, Meyerhold and Grotowski. The book started life as a PhD thesis which I successfully defended in 2004, but which left me unsatisfied because it didn't fully engage with questions of theatre. The thesis laid the two forms of knowledge side by side, rather than bringing them into any kind of dynamic interaction. It took twelve years to realize that the filter for the book was actually quite simple: I could only deal with those aspects of Bakhtin's thinking that bore directly on questions of theatre. Within this framework I could establish a dialogue between these two domains of thinking.

The questions in this present study focus more on the training (I would prefer to say 'formation') of the actor's body, on what actors know (whether or not they *know* they possess this knowledge) and on what can be known about the human body by studying the training and knowledge of the actor's body. The present dialogue is between, on the one hand, a range of scientists, philosophers and researchers in related disciplines, and on the other, theatre practitioners and pedagogues. Questions about the relation between an actor and their role return us to the dialogue between Stanislavsky and Meyerhold started in *Bakhtin and Theatre*. As with that book, indeed in the spirit of Bakhtin, this is a dialogue of inter-illumination between two very different kinds of thinking and writing about the human body. The present book asks some basic questions about the actor's body and how it is 'formed' through different kinds of training. The point of drawing together all these different and often conflicting approaches to the human body is to provoke and propose new ways of thinking about how we use ourselves.

Another important dialogue behind this book have been the conversations I have enjoyed with John Rothwell (professor of the neurophysiology of human movement at the Institute of Neurology, University of London). Over the past ten years we have tried to explain to each other something of what we do: me in the studio, he in the laboratory. We began by having human movement as our point in common and have slowly come to understand each other's work a little better. His answer to most questions I ask is that 'We don't know, indeed I don't know how one could know.' I have been reading about the brain since a child and remember reading an article in a Sunday magazine in the early 1970s where I came across a statement (which I paraphrase from memory): 'So little is known about the brain; it could be powered by elastic bands for all we know.' These friendly correctives remind me of just how little is still known about the workings of the brain and its nervous systems and how one must be careful about pushing the little one does know too far.

Another dialogue has been with cognitive psychologist Phillip Barnard who came to watch me lead a workshop in the 1990s. His comments were illuminating in that he saw processes and strategies in my teaching of which I was entirely unaware. He could describe things I knew but of which I had no conscious knowledge. However, subsequent conversations revealed the gulf between our approaches to research. He pointed out how my questions about cognition and movement were vast, whereas his were extremely specific and narrow. I work at a macro and he at a micro stage. Despite this, he continues to work with theatre practitioners to explore how his specialist knowledge can illuminate aspects of creative practice.

There are many problems and caveats about writing a generalist book about the dialogue between neuroscience and the work of the actor. The human brain is being understood in a way hitherto previously unthought of thanks to ever more precise imaging technology. This has the downside that theories in the rapidly evolving field of neuroscience can become quickly outdated. Another problem is that although some books on neuroscience have the general reader in mind

(Damasio's in particular), many demand specialist knowledge. Although I have read quite a number of books on neuroscience, there is no way that I can offer any kind of informed critique of the scientific thought in those books. From that point of view the dialogue is distinctly one-way. But it would be a poorer world if none of us took a calculated risk in our attempts to understand ourselves and our world. Hopefully the thinking in this book might prompt other researchers to go further than I have been able to do. The use that an actor makes of their body could prompt us to think more generally about how non-actors use theirs. Equally, recent research into how body and brain work together might help actors think differently about their practice and by extension may give non-actors pause for thought. Finally, the non-theorized knowledge of actors might point to physical and psychological phenomena and problems that have not been recognized by neuroscientists and may open new fields of research.

A glance at the acknowledgements will indicate how many people have helped me along the way with this book. One problem for readers of *Rethinking the Actor's Body* might be the amount that I draw on the thoughts and writings of other authors. At times it may seem as if I am writing more as an editor rather than a single author. I take encouragement from the writer Walter Benjamin who dreamed of a book consisting only of quotations! I should alert you to the fact that at times in this book I will play the role of a curator of an imaginary dialogue between thinkers whose ideas may never before have been brought together into the same discussion. In doing this I am trying to demonstrate that there is a possible conversation to be had between neuroscience and theatre practice. That said, this book is far from being a comprehensive compendium of all the different knowledges of the body that could be brought together in order to prompt the reader to think again about the nature and potential of the human body. My book is more a florilegium, a personal anthology of writings that indicate a possible multi-disciplinary approach.

This book starts from the premise that in studying one kind of training of the human body (i.e. actor training) it may be possible to understand more general principles about how we develop and learn. It is fuelled by the hunch that the developing field of neuroscience (and other sciences and philosophies of the body) can offer some useful tools for furthering this understanding. I am offering a hypothesis and not a fully researched and grounded thesis. Call this a work in progress, a call to arms, an invitation to explore an exciting new field of research. I conclude with the inspiring words of Michael Polanyi:

> Yet, looking *forward*, before the event, the act of discovery appears personal and indeterminate. It starts with the solitary intimations of a problem, of bits and pieces here and there which seem to offer clues to something hidden. They look like fragments of a yet unknown coherent whole. This tentative vision must turn into a personal obsession; for a problem that does not worry us is no

problem: there is no drive in it, it does not exist. This obsession, which spurs and guides us, is about something that no one can tell: its content is undefinable, indeterminate, strictly personal. Indeed, the process by which it will be brought to light will be acknowledged as a discovery because it could not have been achieved by any persistence in applying explicit rules to given facts.[1]

---

[1]Polanyi 2009: 75–6.

ACKNOWLEDGEMENTS

I f I mention dialogue in the title of this book it is because it could not have been written without my continuing dialogues with the following people: Campbell Edinborough, John Rothwell, Gary Stevens, Elaine Turner, David Wiles, Rose Whyman, Thomas Wilson, Libby Worth, the late Brian Roberts, and of course, Jonathan Grieve. I cannot thank them enough for their patience and generosity. Matthew Cohen I thank for sharpening the title of this book: 'rethinking' is the perfect word.

I am grateful to John O'Donovan who showed me what a proper editor can do, and to Anna Brewer who has continued to look after me at Methuen Drama. Early versions of this book were read by Caryl Emerson and Kasia Zaremba-Byrne whose comments were so useful and encouraging. The staff at the British Library deserve thanks for their support, help and friendship. I thank my colleagues in the Department of Drama, Theatre and Dance at Royal Holloway, University of London, and reserve my warmest thanks for my students who give me permission to think aloud, and who so creatively engage in my experiments.

PART ONE

INTRODUCTION

Two Images of the Human Body

A remarkable machine unlike any other I had seen before was rushing toward me…. It apparently did not have any wheels but nevertheless moved forward with an amazing speed. As I was able to see, its most important part was a pair of powerful elastic rods each one consisting of several segments … Each rod moved along a complex curved arch and suddenly made a soft contact with the ground. Then it looked as if lightning ran along from the top to the bottom, the rod straightened and lifted off the ground with a powerful, resilient push and rushed upwards again.[1]

I first encountered this extraordinary passage in Scott Kelso's book *Dynamic Patterns* (1995) and imagine that it was quoted so that we could view the moving body with fresh eyes. The alien who beholds a human being walking is struggling to understand how this remarkable machine works. I shall adopt the same kind of detached wonderment as I attempt to understand how actors and performers use their bodies. Of course, as I stated in *Training the Actor's Body* (2018), there is no such thing as an *actor's* body, in the same way there is no such thing as a wine-taster's palate, or a pastry chef's hands. All are simply the products of a very specific training that results in particular competencies and sensitivities. I have written this book in the hope that readers will be able to see the human body (and their own body) with fresh eyes by looking through lens of actor training.

Rethinking the Actor's Body is written for students of theatre and theatre studies; I hope it will also be of interest to practising actors and those specializing in movement for the actor. More broadly, I hope it will be of use to researchers and teachers in the field of theatre practice, and, who knows, to students and researchers working in the field of neuroscience.

Over the course of my book, I shall draw on three ways of understanding the human body. Given the title of this book, the main focus will be on how an actor

---

[1]Scott Kelso 1995: 30–1.

knows their body. The next kind of understanding comes from practitioner/ academics who write about ways of knowing the actor's body. These hybrid figures (like me) look both to practitioner knowledge and to academic theory in order to make sense of performance practice. Amongst these practitioner/ academics there are some who have (again like me) taken an interest in recent neuroscientific research. Finally, I shall cite the writings of philosophers, scientists and neuroscientists which I will argue could help us better understand the function and structure of the actor's body.

There are several historical frames to this study. A background to the whole study is the history of twentieth-century performer training. Bringing us to the present day is the much more recent history of neurophysiology whose rapidly developing understanding of the brain and its nervous systems means that claims made in this book will almost certainly have to be revised in the light of future discoveries. Nested within these two frames are the parallel and occasionally intersecting histories of Russian/Soviet theatre and psychology.

The aim of this book is not to translate the actor's practical know-how into scientific terms, nor to find applications in theatre practice for scientific theories and models. Both these approaches reduce one of the terms. My study will involve a range of different understandings of the actor's body, and thereby expand the different ways that we can grasp the nature and function of this fascinatingly complex organism. I shall draw on recent neuroscientific research to offer ways of thinking about the function and structure of the body which is brought into intelligent action through the activity of the brain and its different nervous systems. Part of this scientific overview will include a sympathetic critique of how neuroscience has been used in recent studies of acting practice and training. Finally, I shall attempt to demonstrate how some aspects of the actor's work can find extension into everyday life. There are lessons for all of us in understanding how the actor learns to use their body.

The second image is that of a human body. My contention in this book is that the envelope of skin which constitutes what we see of the human body contains all that there is to know. I shall cite many authors who write about the embodied self, about embodiment and about the dangers of a dualist approach where the body and mind are conceived as separate entities. I follow this line of thinking and agree that we are one unified structure which cannot be separated into a thinking and a doing part, or an emotional and a rational part. The problem with the seemingly simple statement that the human body is an integrated structure that operates as a whole is that this operation is fantastically complex and is therefore commensurately difficult to understand. Dualism is a seductively simple way of understanding the operation of the human body with its separation between a mind/self and a body. Even when some writers espouse the notion of a unified body, they still write using a dualist model. English grammar makes it hard not to think of two discrete entities when we are obliged to talk about 'my arm, my leg', as if these limbs were the property of an independent self. While accepting how difficult it is to shake off dualist assumptions, this book is about *rethinking* the body, and therefore I see it as part of my job to challenge these deeply ingrained habits of thinking.

Writers like J.A. Scott Kelso (and Andy Clark, Antonio Damasio, Shaun Gallagher and other philosophers and neuroscientists who will be mentioned throughout this book) offer us ways of understanding the bewildering complexity of the human organism. This brings us back to the image with which Scott Kelso begins his book on Dynamic Patterns. Dynamics is a branch of physics which understands the non-linear behaviour of complex systems. There is no more complex system than the human organism, in terms of both its mechanical structures comprising bones, muscles and connective tissues, and its neurological structures, and how they all operate in concert. I shall draw on his thinking to help explain the complexity of the human body in action.

Readers (all of them from a theatre background) of earlier drafts of this book have told me that parts of my argument are too difficult. These are precisely the parts where I have begun to discuss the complex nature and operation of the human body and draw some more general philosophical points from this discussion. Rather than cutting these parts, I have tried to render them as simply as possible, but no simpler (as Einstein was rumoured to have said). Our discussions about the human body must go beyond statements about it being a unified system, and start explaining a little more about how this system actually works. All my discussions are supported by references to easily accessible books (like Scott Kelso's) to which the reader can refer if they want to learn more.

Different Actors, Different Bodies

Just as the notion of 'the body' is an abstraction, so too is the notion of 'the actor's body'. There are as many types of actor's body and as many different kinds of acting as there are different forms of theatre: from pub theatre to West End or Broadway Theatre, from New Writing in the Royal Court Theatre, to immersive theatre, to site-specific theatre, to physical theatre. In all these kinds of theatre, the actor draws on his or her own bodily resources to create distinctly different kinds of performance. Within these different kinds of theatre there are different kinds of actor. John Gielgud would rely on his face and voice, acting, as it were, from his neck upwards; other actors make extravagant use of their physicality and can transform themselves into almost unrecognizable shapes (e.g. Michael Chekhov, Alex Guinness or Toby Jones). Some actors can play across much of the theatrical spectrum, including film and television; others are more specialized.

One opposition that will run through this book is that between a 'psychological' and a 'physical' approach to acting, the first represented by Stanislavsky, the second by his pupil Vsevolod Meyerhold. What do theatre practitioners and commentators mean by the terms 'physical' and 'psychological'? We will discover that behind this opposition there is the equally fundamental (and also equally contested) distinction between an 'inner' and 'outer' approach to acting. Does the impulse or the emotion come from within the actor and then find outer expression in movement, or does the change of the inner state result from the performance of the movement? In both cases, the way the body is understood determines the 'truth' of the movement.

Meyerhold gives a historical dimension to this opposition by claiming that his more physical approach looks to an ancient tradition of performance. Richard Axton lists the names for 'actor' and 'performer' which were used 'by writers in the period between the sixth and fourteenth centuries', noting how it 'is often impossible to distinguish between *mimi* (originally popular entertainers of the Roman "burlesque" theatre), *histriones* (professional actors), *lusores* (players) and *scurri(ae)* (jesters?).'[2] This passage offers an image of theatre and acting that is physical, comic and often vulgar: a theatre of the grotesque body.[3] Certainly, images on ancient pottery dating from the second century BCE found in Southern Italy indicate characters from Atellan Farces – which were most certainly scurrilous – that seem to look forward to Commedia dell' Arte. It is precisely this tradition of physical, popular theatre that Meyerhold draws upon in his modernist challenge to what he regards as Stanislavsky's outdated realism (the 'old theatre' referred to in the next quotation). Meyerhold refers to 'the refined grace, the extreme artistry of the old yet eternally new tricks of the histrions, mimi, atellanae, scurrae, jaculatores and ministrelli', adding that 'the actor of the future should, or if he wishes to remain an actor, *must* co-ordinate his emotional responses with his technique, measuring both against the traditional precepts of the old theatre.'[4]

At about the same time (the mid-1920s) as Meyerhold was developing his Biomechanical approach to actor-training, in France Antonin Artaud was challenging what he regarded as the outdated realism of French literary theatre and demanding a 'physical' theatre which was aimed directly towards the bodily senses of the audience rather than their intellects. This 'new' theatre challenged the architecture and the audience of 'traditional' theatre and championed the expressive potential of the actor's body. As the twentieth century wore on the traditional theatre survived the criticisms from Artaud, Meyerhold and others, and while the practice of physical theatre continued, it was always as an alternative to the more dominant form of realism. There are too many examples of physical theatre to cite here, but certainly the experiments of Jerzy Grotowski in the 1960s and the teaching of Jacques Lecoq in the 1970s and 1980s have each had

---

[2]Axton 1974: 18.
[3]For my earlier thoughts on the grotesque body, see McCaw 2016: 173–4.
[4]Meyerhold 1991: 127.

a massive impact on the production of physical theatre. (Although working in a very different tradition to Meyerhold, Lecoq would also draw on the tradition of Atellan farce and Commedia in his conception of physical theatre.) I would argue that today the dominant mode of theatre production remains realist, text-based theatre. Much debate and evaluation of theatre in the broadcast and written media still focus upon character and how an actor can render such characters believable. For this reason 'character acting' is still central to professional actor training, and thus it is part of this study of the actor's body.

There is broad agreement in literature on acting and actor training that the actor's body is a double thing. An audience might experience sorrow and pain for the character's body and all the injuries to which it is submitted, but 'behind' that body is that of the actor, whose transparent artistry makes minute adjustments of dynamics and rhythm, according to the contours of any particular performance. In physical theatre, where the actor is not necessarily playing a character, there is still a commitment to wholly embody a movement in order to maximize its expressive intent. In all these kinds of theatre one thing is clear: that the actor has to do things with their body which demand a specific kind of technique, which in turn requires its own kind of training. The actor's work may not be as obvious as that of the dancer's, the musician's or the athlete's, but it tunes and transforms the everyday body just as profoundly.

A Study of the Actor's Body Opens on to Other Understandings of the Body

Apart from trying to offer different ways of understanding the actor's body this book is also about rethinking it. The way I use the word 'thinking' (and by extension, 'rethinking') has a great deal to do with Mabel Todd's book *The Thinking Body* (1968) where she argues that very often the way we use of our body is limited or compromised by poor or inaccurate thinking about it. Much of her argument concerns our ignorance of the nature and function of the pelvis and the big muscle groups around it. Such ignorance means that we operate from a misleading image of our bodies – we move *as if* our centre of movement is in the upper rather than the lower body. In order to create a thinking body she argues that we must rethink ourselves, which means creating a more accurate image of how we move. This image will inform and guide our movements and actions.

When authors of books on actor training write about 'the body', they offer their own particular image of its function and structure that is informed by and geared to acting. (This might well be the case in books on sports science.) The authors want the reader to grasp how an everyday body can be trained in any particular field of endeavour. Part of the present book's task is therefore to help the reader understand the different conceptions of the body that can be found in books on actor training, and to explain as far as it is possible what is meant by certain terms and why they are being used. For example, the word 'centre' has a very particular meaning in the actor-training lexicon, as does 'energy', as does the term 'psycho-physical'. To what extent are such terms literal or figurative?

In many ways Clive Barker's *Theatre Games* (2010) is a model for my book. His bibliography indicates his astonishing breadth of reference and research: from the sociology of Roger Caillois's theory of games, to Erwin Goffman's theory of role-play, to the philosophy of Martin Buber which focused on the relation between I and Thou, to movement thinkers like Moshe Feldenkrais and Rudolf Laban. Barker knew very well that acting doesn't consist of a single technique that can be taught and examined in one way. His bibliography is a net of different disciplines in which he hoped to capture that elusive thing called acting. An acting method is judged according to whether it works for a particular actor. I have already noted how acting and actor training are mercilessly pragmatic. This might explain why many books on acting are an eclectic mixture of imagery, personal anecdote and related sciences or practices. Barker makes brilliant and personal use of his reading and thereby arrives at a book that has an enviable balance of practical instruction and theoretical reflection; he has created a conversation between sociology, movement theory and theatre studies. Although the majority of the literature cited in this book comes from the field of actor training, I also refer to three other fields of research.

The first is neuroscience, which has been the subject of theatrical interest for some time, notably Peter Brook's 1993 adaptation of Oliver Sacks's *The Man Who Mistook His Wife for a Hat* (1985). This was produced at the end of a century that had seen the development and flourishing of actor training which from its outset had an important connection with brain sciences, from Stanislavsky's reading of Théodule Ribot (1839–1916) and other psychologists to Meyerhold's correspondence with the behaviourist Ivan Pavlov (1849–1936), each finding a scientific method that was consonant of their image of how body and mind work together. Within the first twenty years of the twentieth century there were two very different accounts of acting each drawing on two correspondingly different kinds of psychology: one focusing on the inner workings of the mind, the other on the outwardly manifested physical behaviour. These were psychoanalysis and behaviourism (which will be discussed in more detail in Chapter 8).

This dialogue between artistic practice and brain sciences is flourishing today. Neurologist Alain Berthoz argues that if the body is to be 'rehabilitated in modern neurobiology, the rules that underlie its movements have to be rediscovered': these are rules which are 'intuitively understood by sculptors who are able to render the movements of the body and their relationship to emotions, as are actors in Asian theatre'. He goes on to explain how these actors 'demonstrate that the kinematics of movement conveys meaning, and that the trajectory of a finger, the displacement of the head, the swaying of the body must respond to laws that are at the crossroads of mechanics and neurology.[5] We should notice that he has written about sculpture and theatre, and that his chosen form of theatre is much closer to the kinds of physical theatre described above. Complementing Berthoz's comments, Joseph Roach notes that 'conceptions of the human body drawn from physiology and psychology have dominated theories of acting from antiquity to the present'.[6] Finally, we find in the preface to Rizzolatti and Sinigaglia's book *Mirrors in the Brain* (2008) a reference to Peter Brook who wonders why it took scientists so long to discover what actors had known all along!

The second disciplinary field is a kind of anthropological sociology that has taken an interest in the physical learning and adaptation of the human body in a social environment. Examples of this research are Tim Ingold's *Being Alive* (2011) and *Making* (2013); Guy Claxton's *Hare Brain, Tortoise Mind* (1997) and *Intelligence in the Flesh* (2015); and Richard Sennett's *The Craftsman* (2008). There is a growing field of cross-disciplinary research which challenges the idea that intellect and knowledge are necessarily the preserve of the thinking self and could be seen as part of an extended body. I shall draw on Claxton and other writers to help understand actor training in a wider context. They describe types of learning and types of knowledge that are analogous to that of acting. They prompt seemingly impossible questions like – What it is that an actor knows and how do they come to know it? Is this knowledge what Claxton calls an 'intelligence in the flesh'? Throughout this book I shall be trying to identify whether there is such a thing as physical intelligence and how it relates to the actor's work, and reversely how the actor's work can shine light on this thing called physical intelligence. Sennett argues that craftwork 'establishes a realm of skill and knowledge perhaps beyond human verbal capacities to explain', and, as an example, challenges the reader to describe how to tie a slipknot. He concludes that 'language is not an adequate "mirror-tool" for the physical movements of the human body.'[7] I take this as a warning as I attempt to account for the different understandings of the actor's body.

Michael Chekhov put this problem quite pithily: 'The training of the body is therefore a training in awareness, in learning how to listen to the body, how to be led by it. […] Words are so clever, but movement is simpler.'[8] This relation between language and learning will be explored in a variety of ways throughout this book. Without wanting to make any grand claims, I hope at least to indicate a new way of doing theory which is shaped and informed by practice. I also hope to demonstrate that a book like Tim Ingold's *Making* (2013) which discusses a very particular kind of embodied knowledge and how it is learned can help us understand the practice of theatre within a broader continuum of human activity.

---

[5]Berthoz 2000: 137.
[6]Roach 1993: 11.
[7]Sennett 2008: 95.
[8]Chekhov in Zarrilli 2009: 20.

Finally, the third field is the kind of developmental training practised by Moshe Feldenkrais and F.M. Alexander. These non-artistic body-oriented methods have informed various kinds of performer training for many years. Peter Brook explains in a letter of 1978 why he invited Moshe Feldenkrais to lead an eight-week workshop at his Centre International de Recherche Théâtral in Paris:

> The very basis of every actor's work is their own body – nothing is more concrete. During the experiments we have made at the International Centre for Theatrical Research we have had occasion to study various techniques which focus on the development of the actor's body, sometimes through dance, sometimes gymnastics, sometimes again through the practice of the martial arts; and it is thus that I have come to know Moshe Feldenkrais.[9]

Brook has elegantly described a whole culture of practical theatre research that was common in the 1970s through until the late 1990s when public funding began to diminish in Western Europe.

In *Theatre & Body* Collette Conroy argues that the body is 'an important area of philosophical investigation' adding that 'the body is a way of thinking about the points of connection between the person and the world'.[10] This sense of connection between world and body is crucial for the argument of this book. In theatre, the body is the point of connection between every element: fellow actors, the spatial set-up of the stage, costumes, properties and, most important of all, the audience. There are two tensions within this book: on the one hand, an effort to focus closely on questions that will enable us to better understand the actor's body, on the other, a desire to demonstrate how these questions inevitably touch on matters of wider interest and fields of application.

Rethinking the Actor's Body: A Book in Two Parts and Nine Chapters

Part One consists of four chapters which examine what I mean by the actor's and the everyday body (which are, of course, the same thing) and how I conceive of the interrelation between brain and body. I also explain my overall methodology for the book. Although this is far from the first book on the connection between the actor's work and neuroscience, its difference lies in how these fields are brought together. At first I thought it might be a question of finding the common area between these two fields:

---

[9]Brook 1978: np.
[10]Conroy 2010: 32.

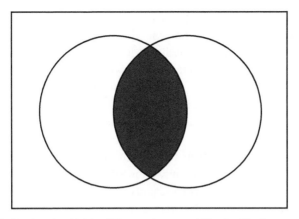

FIGURE I.1 Overlapping Fields of Neuroscience and Theatre Studies.

However, I found the connections much more local and fragmented. There was nothing as simple as one common area, and the gaps or near-connections were just as interesting as the commonalities. My argument thus consists of near-matches of models and terms, places where they seem to touch but are in actuality far apart; I am as interested in the misses as I am in the matches.

Much of the thematic material for the book is introduced in these opening chapters and they will weave throughout the remaining chapters, accumulating new detail and perspectives at each return. Part Two consists of five chapters and concludes with an attempt to demonstrate how what we have learned about the actor's body and brain can have extension into everyday life.

Chapter 1 – Different Ways of Understanding a Body (Methodology)

This is a first take on many subjects to which we will return throughout the book. Divided into three sections, the first will tackle the most general of questions: what is it to be a body? All knowing of and through the body begins not so much through the *fact* but the *act* of being a body. To rethink the body means *not* to take bodily functions like moving and perceiving for granted; they have to become problems again so that we can appreciate the bewildering and wonderful complexity of our bodies. All actors have to rethink their bodies precisely because they are undertaking a new use of their bodies. We can no longer take simple activities like walking, standing up and sitting down for granted; we must rethink the faculties of sensing and of perception and realize that they are not about the passive receptions of impressions of the outside world, but rather active constructions of an image of the world. Geraldine Stephenson, who taught me the basics of movement, would cite a question posed by her teacher, Rudolf Laban: he would ask actors 'How would your character *not* sit down?' This question sets the actor on a path of discovering all the possible ways of sitting down. This shift from passive to active enquiry characterizes the tone of this entire book.

Neuroscientists Tononi and Edelman note the difficulty in this shift of perspective: how can we study states of consciousness when that state is my feeling of myself? Is that sense of being 'me', my conscious mind, somehow different from the body, or is it generated by my body and brain? Here we have another huge question which will resonate throughout the book. Such a dualist approach seems so *natural*. I am not sufficiently knowledgeable about neuroscience to use its arguments to disprove dualist accounts of body and mind, but I will offer some credible alternatives. In the process of rethinking we will discover that the taken-for-granted body is far more complex than we had ever imagined. From my reading of some of the neuroscientific literature it is clear that scientists are just beginning to fathom this complexity.

The second rethinking of the body considered in this chapter has been undertaken by a group of theatre scholars and practitioners who have drawn on their readings of neuroscience to offer insights into the practice and understanding of theatre and performance. Without their initial research my bibliography would be thinner and my thinking poorer and thus I happily acknowledge my debt to them. It is their claim that neuroscience can offer a new, objective approach to the work of the actor that has helped shape my own approach. I am less interested in replacing pre-scientific ways of thinking about the actor's body, as much as examining the assumptions that underpin these ways of thinking.

The third part of this chapter deals with some of the neuroscientific concepts upon which I will draw in my book. The writing and practice of Feldenkrais loom large in this book as they did in *Training the Actor's Body*. So does the thinking of Nikolai Bernstein, who though active in the 1930s and 1940s remains an important figure because of his interdisciplinary approach to understanding how the human body learns fine movement. When I touch on Systems Theory and Dynamic Patterns we encounter another fundamental theme in my book: in order to understand the nature of bodily processes (be they thinking, feeling or moving) we must grasp them as precisely that, *ongoing processes* that unfold over time, rather than as static images (which is the habitual way of grasping an idea). This involves a major shift in our way of thinking and understanding, and as I've already stated, it is more complex. Many of these processes are non-linear and often they are parallel (happening at the same time), thus we need to think in terms of rhythmic loopings rather than straight lines.

The idea of the extended brain questions the habitual notion that there is a world out there and our body in here. Writers like Andy Clark and Scott Kelso suggest the idea of an extended body to explain how we act in and with the world. Perhaps naively, I contend that this model of how we meaningfully extend into our surrounding environment could inform the practice of the performer and actor. The chapter finishes with a review of another kind of literature that has had a profound effect on this book: the writings of Guy Claxton, Tim Ingold and Richard Sennett straddle the fields of philosophy, anthropology and sociology and share the common goal of understanding what we might call a physical, body-based intelligence, precisely the kind of intelligence that I think is possessed by the performer or actor.

Chapter 2 – Training: From the Everyday Body to the Actor's Body

This chapter focuses mostly on the human body in its everyday operation and will tackle basic questions about the structure and function of the human body, including its neurology. Although everyone knows that we are born incapable of purposeful movement, we forget that all of the faculties that we take for granted are in fact created through a long process of self-directed learning. I shall begin by asking why moving organisms need brains, which leads into a more detailed discussion of the function of the sensorimotor system. We need brains to match perceptions of the surrounding world with appropriate motor responses. Examples of very simple organisms present an image of co-being: the nature of our bodies is predicated upon the nature of our surrounding environment (another challenge to dualism).

This returns us to Andy Clark's concept of a brain in a body which 'extends' into the world. The human body constitutes a unique structural adaptation to the world, a way of living the world in a particular way. I will argue that we need to understand some of the principal features of this adapted structure before we can then grasp the significance of the training of the actor's body. Having examined how the human body makes sense of its environment we then move on to how the actor makes sense of the stage environment. This looks forward to parts of Chapter 5 where we will examine the structure of the human spine and how it affords our spatial orientation. The chapter ends with a discussion of skin, muscles and finally feet. (The spine and chest will be discussed in Chapter 4.) Why these three aspects of anatomy? Because they reveal just how much our habitual image of the human body leaves out. These accounts come from a variety of perspectives, mostly from the realm of theatre and performance. The aim of this section is to help us start thinking differently about the structure and the expressive potential of the human body.

Chapter 3 – Front Brain/Back Brain

The next two chapters take their titles from Barker's *Theatre Games*. My use of his distinction between front and back brain (which he took from Feldenkrais's 1949 book *Body and Mature Behaviour*) offers an example of how theatre thinking can be informed by neurological science. We will see that Barker is neither completely wrong nor entirely correct in his thinking, but has adapted current scientific knowledge for his own purposes. His overall approach is underpinned by a modular notion of the brain whereby a specific part of the brain is associated with a function, a notion that denies the fundamental complexity of the brain which operates (as stated above) through complex time-based looping patterns. This will be our first example of how we need to understand human activity dynamically rather than statically. We will also confront two other difficult ideas: firstly, that our actions are not the playing out of motor programmes, and furthermore that they are not guided by a little person inside our head (another dualist notion). While Barker's is a simplified and static account of the brain, there is a fundamental truth that the front brain does process reflective cogitation while back and lower brain functions deal with movement.

Much of the neurological literature seems agreed that we are conscious of about 5 per cent of our brain's activity. This is not due to any lack of attention on our part, but because (a) there are many neural activities that are not accessible to conscious attention, (b) because conscious attention would slow down otherwise non-conscious activities and (c) because we can only consciously attend to one process at a time. Barker describes 'the core of Stanislavski's method' as being 'the translation of conscious intention into subconscious action'.[11] This leads to two separates strands of discussion. The first concerns states of attention, which Barker describes with peculiar acuity. The second lies in the meaning of the terms 'unconscious', 'non-conscious' and 'subconscious'. Thus we will examine how an actor's knowledge has to become invisible (non-conscious) and how the actor's spontaneity relies on instinctive reactions of which they are not 'directly conscious'. These themes are then expanded into a broader discussion of consciousness, awareness and effective action.

Chapter 4 – 'Body/Think': Being, Sensing, Knowing

Barker's notion of body/think[12] is his expression for our kinaesthetic sense.

> Ease of mobility around the central axis of the body implies that the actor is the centre of his own personal area of space, to which all other objects and people in space relate. I have argued that this is the natural condition of the human being; and that the kinaesthetic use of the body/think tends to reinstate it.[13]

---

[11]Barker 2010: 17.
[12]Barker 2010: 29, 126–8, 137–8, 160.
[13]Barker 2010: 137.

I only quote at this length because the first sentence gives a preview of much of the argument of Chapter 6, concerned as it is with the notion of a centre, both figuratively and in the literal sense that Barker uses, as our central axis of turning. In a brilliant turn of argument he presents this axial mobility as being the 'natural condition of the human being' which is reinstated (in the actor) through developing the kinaesthetic sense. I shall discuss some elements of the neurology of the kinaesthetic sense (and of proprioception), without repeating earlier or encroaching upon the arguments of later chapters.

We know ourselves thanks to the suite of senses with which every neuro-typical body is equipped, and which extend far beyond the classic five senses, and include the already-mentioned proprioceptive and kinaesthetic senses. The first part of the chapter will examine how the actor's body requires considerable development of what one might call sensorimotor sensitivity: this is not simply a question of being able to pick up more sensory data but being able to translate this raw data into meaningful information. In short, it is a process of making sense of your senses. How does the actor develop these senses in their work on stage? Much of this part of the chapter will look back to *Training the Actor's Body* (2018) where I describe the project of the book as being a development of our sensitivity.[14] In the earlier book my concern was how to develop this sensitivity through training: the present book will examine the physiological means by which it is achieved.

In *Training the Actor's Body* I also argued that 'the knowledge' an actor acquires through training 'could equally be called a sensitivity, a perceptual capacity, a capacity for feeling'.[15] In this book I will examine how several philosophers have described this kind of knowledge, particularly Gilbert Ryle whose distinction between knowing 'what' and knowing 'how' looks forward to Michel Polanyi's notion of tacit knowledge. (Once again returning us to the opposition between faculties that are invisible and those that are visible.) The argument brings us back to the central problem of action, for as Dewey observed, 'Popular terms denoting knowledge have always retained the connection with ability in action lost by academic philosophies.'[16] He points out the relation between 'ken' and 'can' and how 'mind' is also a verb conveying the sense of care (as in, child minding). I shall argue that this connection between doing and knowing is one way of grasping the nature of embodied knowledge.

The chapter finishes with a double problem: how can the actor or performer access this knowledge so that it becomes 'second nature', but avoids this 'tacit knowledge' becoming mechanically reproduced habit? Although Drew Leder and others argue that the body becomes invisible or absent in action, I argue that an actor cannot allow this to be the case. This last point returns us to the opposition

---

[14]McCaw 2016: 10–11.
[15]McCaw 2016: 3.
[16]Dewey 2004: 178.

between machine and organism that will recur throughout my argument. I shall argue that Barker's notion of back-brain attention may offer a means whereby the actor can avoid repeating a performance or slipping into bad habits. The chapter thus begins with theatre theory, which is then tested against neuroscientific theory which in turn is shown to provide an insufficient account of theatre practice, which finally offers a possible solution to the problem of how one can act with awareness.

Chapter 5 – A Present Body

How is it that some actors can hold our attention without doing anything? What is it about their physical presence that holds our attention or attracts our curiosity? If the answer concerns the performer's energy or *bios* (Eugenio Barba's term), then how are we to understand such a term? How is energy discussed and described in actor-training literature, and how might one make sense of these descriptions? Are they literal or figurative?

These questions are at the centre of an actor's understanding of their body but how would one begin to explain such concerns to a non-performer? Is this energy of presence solely confined to the stage and performance, or is it found in everyday life, as in the expression 'She lit up a room whenever she entered it'. Can the performer's energy be accounted for in neurophysiological or neurobiological terms? The chapter charts a history of psychophysical acting from work in Stanislavsky's First Studio in the early 1900s through the researches of Grotowski in the 1960s and then to more recent studies.

Chapter 6 – Figuring the Body

How can one make sense of the actor's body through its sense of orientation in space? This primary sense of orientation enables healthy humans to move in space, and by extension to understand the movement of others, and underlies many higher forms of sense-making. As with other chapters, the argument will alternate between the figural terms in actor training and more scientific language. My major enquiry will be into the concept of a centre. Many actors make use of this term, which is probably drawn from the everyday sense 'to concentrate in, on. To be centred in or on' (*OED*). I shall ask whether the concept of a 'centre' can make sense of the actor's body or the way it moves. Is there a meaningful distinction between acting that begins with an internal impulse which then finds outward expression, and acting that begins with an external movement which then seeks for internal resonance and justification? In this chapter I shall explore the literal and the figurative significance of the notion of a bodily centre, be it the central axis around which we move (head, spine, pelvis), or more metaphorical notions of inside-out or outside-in, or even the Eastern notion of centres of energy (bringing us back to the concerns of Chapter 4). In part, this chapter offers 'present-ness' as another way of understanding the actor's presence in space. It could be seen as a counterpart to Chapter 7 which also focuses on a variety of conceptions of the body and its operation.

Chapter 7 – Imaging the Body

Here we explore yet another variation on the theme of inside and outside perspectives of the body. I shall explore two related ideas: the faculty of imagination and the nature of an image. Is it helpful for the actor to imagine what they look like? We will see Stanislavsky at the mirror, Michael Chekhov work on his characters by fully imagining them (how they walk, speak, dress), and Meyerhold ask his actors to be aware of themselves as plastic figures in space (looping back to the concerns of Chapter 5). This opens out into a wider discussion about the role of imagination in the actor's work, and whether this has connection with the claim (made by several neurophysiologists, notably Alain Berthoz) that one of the main functions of the brain is to create simulations. The 'inside/outside' debate will turn on the value of such an external perspective: is it superficial, does it lead to self-consciousness? The alternative approach would be to focus on inner feelings, rather than outer images. Should the body be trained to become an instrument of feeling, or, to use Artaud's remarkable expression, to become a 'fine nerve metre'? Actors cannot know themselves solely through their visual sense: it is only through the 'inner' sense of proprioception that they can grasp themselves as a whole.

Chapter 8 – The Emotional Body

In trying to discover how an actor accesses emotion we bring back into play a number of familiar themes and distinctions, principal amongst which is the inside-out, outside-in opposition. Simply put, do authentic emotions come from the actor's memory, from their imagination, or is it generated through performing appropriate actions? The actor has a unique perspective on emotion, since (developing upon the argument of Chapter 1) they have to find a means of recreating an emotion night after night. Although it would be foolhardy (simpler to say 'impossible') to suggest I have an answer as to how they do this, I shall discuss different theories, proposed both by actors and by practitioner-theorists.

This long chapter divides into three parts. The first concerns debates within theatre about how emotions are accessed. This will be the last iteration of the dialogue between Stanislavsky and Meyerhold about acting and theatre. We will see how both drew on the neuroscientific ideas of their today to support their own theory of acting. Much of their dialogue took place in the first twenty years of the Russian Revolution where not only political structures were overthrown but every theory and institution within the sciences and the humanities. We will see how Stanislavsky's notions of acting and theatre suffered in the early days of the Revolution but became the basis for Socialist Realist Theatre. In the arguments that raged in the fields of theatre and neuroscience key words were 'emotion' and 'consciousness' as practitioners deliberated whether the truth lay in first-person experience or in observed behaviour.

If emotion is a problematic subject in the field of theatre, it is equally so in the field of neuroscience. The second part of this chapter will draw on neuroscientific theories that might help us understand some of the debates about the nature of emotion in Part One. Joseph Ledoux has written books (1998, 2002) on emotion and argues how the subject has been ignored by cognitive scientists and other neurologists. This despite Antonio Damasio's pioneering research which demonstrates that decision-making is quite as much about emotion as it is about reason. Damasio is one of the few neurologists to include discussion of an actor's work in his books. Although this chapter will draw on a wide range of theories, these will be deployed in an attempt to account for how the actor's body is employed to generate emotion in performance.

We then turn to a very different kind of emotion. For some actors stage fright threatens their capacity to act, while for others it is an essential spur to energetic performance. Stanislavsky writes with great feeling about his stage fright and his attempt to devise a technique whereby the actor can remain relaxed when in the intensely stressful situation of performance. An analysis of his ideas will lead to an exploration of the structure and function of the autonomic nervous system and explore how one branch of the system is accelerative (producing the 'fight, flight, freeze' reaction) while the other is decelerative (and is at the heart of practices like yoga, meditation and tai chi).

Chapter 9 – Bringing It All Back Home

Throughout this book I have examined terms and concepts coming from within the field of acting and performance, and from other fields that I thought would be helpful in trying to better understand the 'actor's body'. The book began by arguing that this body is a development of the body that every actor is born with; it is a skilled body in the way that a pastry chef's fingers are the same fingers they were born with, but over years of training and practice have become endowed with an acutely developed sense of touch, and facility for fine movement. In this final chapter I shall sketch out some lines of extension from the field of drama into the realms of practical living and philosophy, as well as formulating some questions that might prompt neurophysiological research. With an emphasis upon action and doing, it should come as no surprise that I shall argue that the practical and philosophical are mixed: my discussions of books by Claxton, Ingold, Polyani,

Ryle and Sennett all focus upon a philosophy of doing, a form of thinking, a way of knowing, a type of knowledge, that all start with doing and refining how we do.

The first major theme concerns wholes. While more philosophically oriented writers (Claxton in particular) argue for a materialist conception of the body as an integrated whole, actors approach the question in practical terms: how can they fully embody a character, how can they act with their whole body? Feldenkrais argues for a bodily practice where the whole body is involved in a movement (letting uninvolved parts be inactive so as not to affect the active parts). While the term 'mindbody' is used by theatre practitioners, I have suggested that this still perpetuates a split, and moreover gives too much prominence to the conscious mind. As noted above, so much of our mental and physical activity is conducted non-consciously. We need to grasp where the mind can be usefully engaged, and where it gets in the way of effective action. I argue that we might become more effective in our action if we knew a little more about how it is that we move and take action. To understand ourselves as moving beings, we need to adopt a dynamic rather than a static mode of analysis. While a dynamic process unfolding over time is harder to grasp than a static once-and-for-all image (a snap-shot), it is our job to explain the importance of processes that unfold over time. We limit ourselves by comparing the mind to a computer which operates the machine of the body: the human organism has neither software nor hardware, both of which develop together through the process of doing. The idea of the mind-operator and the body-machine is hard to dispel, but it stops us from grasping the exquisite complexity of us as living and moving beings.

Part of this chapter will be a plea, not so much for Clark's Extended Body, but a body that is simply more of itself: more aware of itself in action in the world and in relation to other people, a body more vital, more sensitive, more alert, more apt to learn. I shall argue (following Feldenkrais) that we can learn more when we grasp how it is we learn, to which I shall add how we can learn from our practice, from our attentive doing. Drawing on the discussion of fear in Chapter 8 I shall argue how we can learn more effectively and perform what we have learned more confidently and fluently when we understand how to manage our anxiety. Related to all the concerns mentioned in this paragraph is the task of achieving a state of optimal attentiveness.

Part of an actor's work is to model how it is that we act in certain circumstances. Many neurophysiologists have argued that one major function of the brain is to simulate actions and movements. They argue that empathy is a kind of cognitive simulation in which one actively imagines oneself in another person's situation. I shall suggest that this kind of modelling has application to a wide variety of problem-solving. We all have bodies that function in unique ways. I hope by looking at the peculiar work of the actor and performer we will understand ourselves a little more clearly. It is to the relation between the actor's and the everyday body that we now turn in Chapter 1.

1 DIFFERENT WAYS OF UNDERSTANDING A BODY (METHODOLOGY)

I To Be a Body

Introduction

> It is only through existing in bodily form that I am what I am. It is through the body that I perceive myself, other persons and things that make up the world. It is through the agency of my body that I am able to act upon them and conversely it is by virtue of my being bodily that they are able to act upon me. When I make the claim that I am a body I mean that it is constitutive of my conscious being in the world. Without my living body I would not exist. It is to this general thesis of bodily being that the term 'embodiment' is given.[1]

The quotation that began the Introduction took the objective, third-person perspective of an admiring alien. Peter Arnold's statement above comes from the very heart of personal experience, where to be is an embodied fact, the very foundation of selfhood. These two quotations describe the breadth of understandings of the body that will be discussed in this book, from detached objectivity to engaged subjectivity. (This is another variation of the theme inside/outside.) Where Scott Kelso's study offers a new way of understanding the moving body as a dynamic organism, Arnold's offers a description of the experience of being an embodied self. This is *my* rather than *a* body 'which is objectively known in terms of scientific datum as it may be to the doctor or dentist'; to me this body 'is a mode of orientation rather than a conceptual abstraction'.[2] In this distinction between 'mode of orientation' and 'conceptual abstraction' lies one of the main arguments of this book. I am interested in the intelligence of our human

---

[1]Arnold 1979: 1.
[2]Arnold 1979: 70–1.

body and how we orientate ourselves in space. Chapter 6 will explore how this spatial orientation can be understood from both an egocentric and an allocentric perspective, that is, one which relies upon an experiencing subject and the other which is independent of 'me'.

The argument thus far has focused on being and existence: knowing that I am because I am a body. John Dewey adds another dimension to the argument when he states, 'An ounce of experience is better than a ton of theory simply because it is only in experience that any theory has vital and verifiable significance.'[3] In writing this Dewey reminds us that the body is not only a thing to be understood (by a third person), but also that with which we understand, and which thereby yields meaning of value.

However Scott Kelso and Arnold are not necessarily at opposite poles since both of them accept that the embodied self is a constantly changing and always moving entity. The difficulty of understanding living organisms is that they are never still. The great movement analyst Warren Lamb loved telling the story of when he was trying to teach a student to observe a person's movement behaviour in a station. After an hour he asked what she had noted. She replied how difficult it had been because the subject kept moving. We are not dealing with 'abstract conceptions' but a body which in its meaningful orientation in space is constantly moving. Trying to describe these processes of change and movement – the subject of Scott Kelso's book – is fiendishly difficult, precisely because we aren't dealing with fixed states. This distinction between static and dynamic is another major theme in this book.

Arnold notes, 'A self is not given ready-made at the beginning.' Neither the sportsperson about whom he is writing nor the actor begins with bodies that are 'ready-made at the beginning'. Both are arrived at through a slow process of training. Arnold continues that the only thing given at the beginning is 'a field of possibility', and we have to track a subject as they project themselves into this particular 'possibility rather than that one'[4] and thus begin to determine who they will become, actor or sportsperson or whomever.

In Arnold's opening quotation he states that to be a body is 'constitutive of my conscious being in the world'. In the context of the actor's body we need to examine what precisely is meant by the word 'conscious'. Of what actions and bodily states does the actor need to be conscious? When is it useful and when unuseful for the actor to be conscious of their activity? How is one conscious of bodily states and changes of state? Related to these questions is the notion of a body that is sometimes 'absent', or 'invisible' in action (absent or invisible to our conscious

---

[3]Dewey 2004: 138.
[4]Arnold 1979: 39.

attention). Although not our direct concern, a discussion of such matters cannot help but touch on an even bigger question: the relation of body and mind.

For over a century, actors, directors and commentators have tried to understand the operation of the body in the context of theatre by drawing on various theories – be they drawn from philosophy or psychology. Stanislavsky was in contact with a variety of Russian and French psychologists, and his student Meyerhold corresponded with the great Soviet physiologist Ivan Pavlov. These two actor/director/teachers were trying to understand how the psychological theories of their time could help them better understand the specific challenges and competencies of the actor's body. Central to understanding this operation are such questions as: How does an actor overcome stage fright? How does one achieve a state of relaxation on stage? How does one achieve an optimal state of concentration? What kind of attentional state does the actor require?

Consciousness: Mind and Body

In their book *A Universe of Consciousness* neuroscientists Edelman and Tonini examine the dilemma with which this chapter opened: does one know what is to be a human from a first- or third-person perspective? They discuss the seeming contradiction of being scientists (who traditionally take a third-person perspective) whose object of study is consciousness (which is a first-person experience). Whereas scientists are usually detached from their object of study, in this case they are dealing with what it is that makes me *me*, the very foundation of being a self. They admit, 'We cannot therefore tacitly remove ourselves as conscious observers as we do when we investigate other scientific domains,'[5] and then go further by stating that 'our conscious experience is the only ontology of which we have direct experience.'[6] Their insistence upon direct experience as a source of understanding of the body is obviously critical to a book about the actor's body. Edelman and Tononi's discussion of conscious experience returns us to the central problem of whether one should understand the body from the outside or inside, and to the related problem of whether we can separate mind (inner self) from body (outer self). The very word 'embody' suggests such a split.

In John Lutterbie's pioneering book *Toward a General Theory of Acting*, he argues that the word 'embodied' 'is not ideal', and suggests we use Sheets-Johnstone's term the 'mind-full body' since 'it recognises that the mind is integrated into physical being, not a separate being'.[7] Cartesian dualism argues precisely that the mind is a separate being made of non-physical stuff. In *Embodiment*

---

[5]Edelman and Tononi 2000: 13.
[6]Edelman and Tononi 2000: 35.
[7]Lutterbie 2011: 24.

and *Cognitive Science* (2005) Raymond Gibbs observes, 'This bifurcation of the person into mind and body has subsequently given rise to so many other dualisms, including subjective as opposed to objective knowledge, knowledge as opposed to experience, reason as opposed to feeling, theory as opposed to practice, and verbal as opposed to nonverbal.'[8] Philosopher Mark Johnson lists a few more dichotomies: 'cognition/emotion, fact/value, knowledge/imagination, and thought/feeling' which are so 'deeply embedded in our Western ways of thinking that we find it almost impossible to avoid framing our understanding of mind and thought dualistically.'[9]

Johnson is one of the few writers who actually explains this split as being an almost inevitable outcome of how we experience ourselves. He explains how 'our bodies hide themselves from us in their very acts of making meaning and experience possible. The way we experience things appears to have a dualistic character. Ironically, it is the nature of our bodies and brains that gives rise to this experience of a split (mental plus physical) self.'[10] Bruce McConachie argues that this split-ness enables us to 'float above the messiness of material reality'.[11] Through our imagination we can transcend our immediate situation in time and space and think ourselves into the future or the past, or into non-existent worlds. One of the actor's greatest gifts is their imagination by means of which they can give body to a character. This is a development of the empathy – the ability to put oneself into another person's shoes – that all of us possess to differing degrees. The very fact that we can talk about knowing our own bodies suggests that somehow we can detach ourselves from bodily selves, or at least reflect upon our states of body.

The dualism of mind and body seems to be an irresolvable conundrum. This is especially concerning given that the work of the actor is with their own bodies. Even to say that 'their bodies are instruments of expression' is dualist in its conception. Scott Kelso and others argue that such functions as consciousness, perception and thought can be understood as dynamic systems within the brain. In this conception of the body and brain there is no simple linearity such as perception-action or stimulus-response. These philosophers and scientists do not conceive of the body and brain as complex computers or machines but rather as infinitely more complex biological organisms whose operation is self-organizing and unpredictable. In this conception the mind (or the self) is not assigned a specific place in the brain but is considered to be a product of that organ in action. Although I stand by a materialist conception of the brain and the body I still find it hard to grasp the idea that mind and consciousness are the result of

---

[8]Gibbs 2005: 4.
[9]Johnson 2007: 7.
[10]Johnson 2007: 4.
[11]McConachie 2013: 2.

vastly complex operations that have taken place within the brain and its associated nervous systems. Such a standpoint holds that there is only the body and that there is no ghost in the machine, no little person in the brain watching the film of our lives, no immaterial and therefore eternal mind.

It is a dizzying shift to consider the mind as a function distributed across neural highways, a shift that removes the possibility of our having an executive centre from which all commands issue. This also challenges much thinking about the actor's body which is understood in terms of a centre from which movements issue and to which sensations report. Even the materialist director Meyerhold writes about the mind being like a machine-operator issuing instructions to the machine-body; although the metaphor is different, it is still based on dualist assumption. I regret that I am unqualified to answer the conundrum that Edelman and Tononi propose at the beginning of this section. I propose a pragmatic strategy whereby we accept the material unity of the human organism (there are no mind and body) but that our consciousness can create the illusion of us being able to separate ourselves from our bodies. Given the subtitle of this book, I shall further propose that we use recent neuroscientific research to illuminate questions and problems of acting and performance.

Knowledges of the Body

In the section above we saw how Edelman and Tononi begin their book on consciousness by pointing out two ways of knowing the human body: the scientist knows 'the body' objectively, whereas we know our bodies through our experience of them, that is, subjectively. I will argue that we know the human body in the first, second and third person.

First-person experience senses what is going inside myself. As you read this page you can become aware of how you are sitting, whether your legs are crossed, or one hand is resting by your side: you know without having to look and check. This faculty for knowing about your body's posture and position in space is called proprioception. Say you then decide to get up and make a cup of tea: your feeling of yourself in motion is called the kinaesthetic sense. Throughout this book I shall explore how it is that we develop these senses of ourselves, whether moving or at rest.

Our next knowledge of the body is in the second person, a rather unrecognized form of knowing. This is the knowledge gained from the physical touch of a therapist – e.g. a physiotherapist or a Feldenkrais practitioner, also a movement teacher or fellow performer. There is a form of educated touch which can bring two human bodies into a mutual understanding of each other. To yield more developed meanings this touch requires training, but maybe it is no more than a development of the interpersonal touch of the parent and the lover.

Finally, one can understand the body from the third-person perspective. We all engage in people watching, developing our theories of what might be going on inside the heads of people as they sit or walk in their own peculiar ways. We make inferences about activity within the head from what we see in their bodies. This faculty of picking up significant details can be developed, and many actors are rather skilled movement observers. They know about the movement of others having spent hours watching them move. Then there are experts like Warren Lamb whose approach is based on objective categories of movement that can be measured: these categories are, as it were, a fine theoretical mesh in which they aim to catch a person's unique movement pattern. While an actor might not know how they know about the movement of a person, Lamb could explain his method with great technical precision.[12] His results and measurements are repeatable. Scott Kelso similarly offers a richly complex account of the process of human movement.

II Theatre Studies Drawing on Neuroscience

Proceeding with Caution

I have already stated that I am not attempting to translate theatrical understandings into scientific terminology. I take both forms of understanding seriously, even if their approaches and languages are different. As Berthoz stated above, it is important that both learn from each other. However, we should heed a warning from Eugenio Barba. He regards the idea that scholars can superimpose 'paradigms which have provided their utility in other fields of research' onto theatre as 'deceitful', and 'based on a superstitious mental attitude' because it claims that such theoretical paradigms have a validity in themselves and thus can be transferred to other contexts willy-nilly. In the context of this book, the 'other fields of research' are 'neuroscience' whose concepts and paradigms will not be transferred to theatre practice 'willy-nilly'. He concedes, 'Interpretative schemas which are valid in one specific context *can* be applied elsewhere. However, the pertinence of such applications must be proved each time.'[13] Neuroscience will teach us nothing if we cannot establish the pertinence of our application to theatre studies.

The past fifteen or so years have seen the emergence of a group of theatre researchers, academics and practitioners who have taken inspiration from recent research in the field of neuroscience. Bruce McConachie conceives of a partnership 'between scientists and scholars in the arts, where both sides can benefit from each other's knowledge.'[14] Introducing her collection of essays *Affective Performance and*

---

[12]See my book *An Eye for Movement* (2006) with accompanying DVD ROM.
[13]Barba 1993: 44.
[14]McConachie 2008: 16.

Cognitive Science: Body, Brain, Being (2013) Shaughnessy suggests that to arrive at such a mutually beneficial partnership one should avoid 'hierarchical, top-down approaches whereby "hard" science is used to validate "soft" performance practice'.[15] She is also alert to what Raymond Tallis calls 'neuromania' which refers 'to reductive, simplistic, misappropriations of scientific theory which overlook the complexities, differences and uniqueness of being human'.[16] Amy Cook makes a similar point that 'performance studies should not simply "use" research from the sciences to "validate" our theories' and that arts researchers should not 'abandon the authority of our knowing'.[17] My aim will be to respect both the 'authority of our knowing' in the performing arts and, as Lutterbie puts it, 'the complexity and wonder of the art form'.[18] I agree with Lutterbie that we should not expect science to 'provide us with answers, but with a way of reframing our understanding of acting that offers a more useful and dynamic way of talking about the actor's art'.[19] The perspective of his book is to 'look across the divide that separates the disciplines and to identify those theories that are based on the most solid evidence and to evaluate their usefulness to understand acting'.[20]

McConachie explains that when drawing on neuroscientific research into cognition, these insights can be subjected to 'empirical investigation', in a way that the 'propositions of poststructuralists such as Michel Foucault, Jacques Lacan, and Jacques Derrida are not falsifiable'. He goes on to explain that the dominance of poststructuralism in the humanities over the past forty years means that 'few theatre and performance scholars have bothered to learn anything about breakthroughs in the cognitive sciences that might challenge their assumptions about what theatre is and how it works'.[21] Elsewhere, he and Elizabeth Hart point how cognitive science 'tends toward realism' which steers between the relativism of poststructuralists and the subjectivism of phenomenologists (which relies on the first-person description of conscious experience). They argue 'consciousness is ill equipped to reveal the operations of the cognitive *unconscious*. Nonetheless, phenomenological insights, impressionistic though they are, can open up important questions for a rigorous cognitive approach to performance.'[22]

Sutton and Tribble point out that 'cognitive science' (which they put in scare quotes) is not some 'monolithic entity', indeed though a 'convenient shorthand [it] is not a meaningful term on its own'. They describe it as 'an interdisciplinary and multidisciplinary field, riven by internal tensions and disagreements, and

---

[15]Shaughnessy 2013: 11.
[16]Shaughnessy 2013: 13.
[17]Amy Cook in Shaughnessy 2013: 55.
[18]Lutterbie 2011: 5.
[19]Lutterbie 2011: 73.
[20]Lutterbie 2011: 74.
[21]McConachie 2013: 6.
[22]McConachie and Hart 2006: 6.

encompassing a wide range of disciplinary perspectives, many of which are not obviously compatible one with another.'[23] Amy Cook points to a similar level of disagreement amongst experts in the field of neurophysiology: a recent symposium found 'competing claims and counterclaims around mirror neurons'.[24] Cook's scepticism is not shared by other writers: Blair argues, 'Mirror neurons allow us to grasp the minds of others not through conceptual reasoning but through direct simulation. By feeling, not by thinking.'[25] Sofia describes 'mirror neurons as the *basic brain mechanism* [...] connecting sensory information with the motor system'. Echoing Blair, she states, 'Our motor system shapes not only our actions but also our perception and therefore our cognition. This is what we call *embodied cognition.*'[26] McConachie and Hart argue that mirror neurons are behind an audience's empathetic observation, which they describe as a 'mode of cognitive engagement involving mirror neurons in the mind/brain that allow spectators to replicate the emotions of a performer's physical state without experiencing that physical state directly'.[27] Suffice it to say that the related fields of cognitive science and neurophysiology are in a state of constant change, fuelled by recent discoveries thanks to new brain imaging technology. Whatever claims we make as non-experts in the field of neuroscience should be made with the utmost care and humility.

Language, Objectivity and Embodied Meaning

Another aspect of the inherent interdisciplinarity of the cognitive sciences (and this book) is that of language and terminology. Blair argues that a 'fundamental challenge of working interdisciplinarily and, often, multimodally lies with language'.[28] There are two aspects to this statement: firstly, that the unilinear unfolding of language (a line of speech unfolding in time, a written line extending in space) cannot represent the unfolding of a multimodal process (which characterizes most organic process); secondly, that the same term can have different meanings according to the discipline in which it is used. We will see how practitioners and commentators argue that the 'fuzzy' thinking of theatre can be sharpened by drawing on the clear thinking of neuroscientists.

Blair argues that an '"acting-targeted" knowledge of how the mind works provides a more concrete vocabulary and set of tools for the actor to use in rehearsal and performance'.[29] The phrase 'concrete vocabulary' is echoed by

---

[23]Sutton and Tribble 2013: 28.
[24]Cook in Shaughnessy 2013: 84.
[25]In Blair 2008:14.
[26]Sofia 2013: 174.
[27]McConachie and Hart 2006: 5.
[28]Blair in Shaughnessy 2013: 136.
[29]Blair 2008: 4.

Kemp who argues three benefits of drawing on cognitive science: teachers will have a 'sound conceptual structure for their work'; practitioners a 'more precise vocabulary for communicating with one another'; and scholars 'more reliable tools' for their analyses of performance and genre.[30] Lutterbie writes admiringly of a study into the origin of concepts because thereby 'scientific methods will eventually transform fuzzy questions into testable ones'.[31] All these adjectives – concrete, sound, precise, reliable, not 'fuzzy' – are used to suggest that the language of theatre (as used by practitioners and commentators) is lacking any of these positive attributes.

In short, the scientific approach is objective rather than subjective, and as a result has, as Blair puts it, 'the potential to feel less "loaded" in personal terms, because its ground is the general process by which all human beings work', rather than focusing on the individual psyche of the performer.[32] Kemp echoes Blair's point when he argues that one advantage of using cognitive science as a foundation for a theory of acting is that it is 'derived from empirical research into human behaviour and is not entangled in the subjective terminology of competing theatrical schools of thought'.[33] Blair concedes that while a cognitive approach 'will not completely demystify what we do when we act', she hopes it 'will change the sense of what and where the mystery is in the process'.[34] According to these writers, theatre practice and theory lack rigour and precision in both its language and its overall methodology. Theatre 'fails' according to Lutterbie because of an inadequate understanding 'of how acting works, a misunderstanding that arises from an inaccurate understanding of the actor's instrument and what it means to be embodied'.[35] Moreover, Lutterbie argues that because 'the body continues to be defined according to binaries' such as inner/outer, emotion/reason, mind/body, it is 'difficult if not impossible to conceive of the human organism holistically'.[36] He argues that such a limited form of thinking is 'crippling when engaged in the art and craft of acting'.[37] Conceiving of the human organism holistically leads onto the question of how meaning can be embodied.

The above writers agree with McConachie that the mind is embodied. 'Not only must the mind work within a living body, but the ways we think – our sense of self and the foundational concepts we use to perceive the world and other people in it – derive from the embeddedness of our bodies on planet earth.'[38] This

---

[30]Kemp 2012: 19.
[31]In Lutterbie 2011: ix–x.
[32]Blair 2008: 4.
[33]Kemp 2012: 94–5.
[34]Blair 2008: 24.
[35]Lutterbie 2011: 22.
[36]Lutterbie 2011: 23–4.
[37]Lutterbie 2011: 24.
[38]McConachie 2013: 1–2.

emphasis upon the embodied mind is echoed throughout the writings of Blair, Kemp and others. An embodied mind means an end to any split between body and mind and, argues Blair, thereby enables performers to 'develop a more accurate picture of themselves as being already necessarily integrated'.[39] She points to how instructions like 'get out of your head' or 'don't think, do' are rooted in a mind-body dualism.[40] Returning to the theme of dualism, Cook explains how 'Our language reflects (and thus rehearses and repeats) the Cartesian split of heart and mind, mind and body. One reason to bring humanities scholars together with scientists is to improve the language use on both sides of the academic split.'[41] The body is thus the site of both the rift and the bridge between science and art, between body and mind.

These writers acknowledge the enormity of their task: they are pioneering an approach to understanding drama based on the findings of groundbreaking research into the human brain and its operation. Kemp writes of his book being part of a 'significant shift in the understanding, theory, and practice of acting', and although it may be 'an ambitious goal', it is one 'justified by the magnitude of the changes in the understanding of the human mind that have led to the concept of the embodied mind'.[42] He explains how 'the mind is inherently embodied, not just in the sense that the brain operates in a body, but because physical experience shapes conceptual thought', noting how the term 'bodymind' is increasingly being used to describe this 'phenomenon'[43] and that this 'holistic concept' will 'support practices that embrace the reflexive and integrated relationship between physicality, thought, emotion, and expression'.[44] Kemp states that one of the aims of his book is to 'make theatre people more aware of what their conceptual understanding of the body is, and to include more scientific knowledge on that understanding', adding that a 'conceptual understanding of the body will influence what one believes it to be capable of'.[45] He offers a conjecture as to the connection 'between physical action and conceptual thought': 'there is neural circuitry from the premotor cortex to other, non-motor domains, which allows the networks that control movement to be used by conceptual domains such as emotion, sensing, and thinking'.[46] Although he admits that this is conjecture, he offers no hint of any possible evidence for it.

---

[39]Blair 2008: 17.
[40]Blair 2008: 26.
[41]Cook in Shaughnessy 2013: 83.
[42]Kemp 2012: 18.
[43]Kemp 2012: xvi.
[44]Kemp 2012: xv.
[45]Kemp 2012: 138.
[46]Kemp 2012: 116.

A Friendly Critique

All the above writings are situated on the border between practice and theory, between art and science, the very territory that I propose to explore. They are a further elaboration to the dilemma discussed at the beginning of this chapter: does one write from the body (in the first person) or about the body (in the third person)? Their research has been invaluable in the conception and writing of this book: they have suggested studies and authors of whose existence I was ignorant, and their thinking has helped me define my own particular set of interests. This debt should be born in mind when reading the critique that follows: I am simply building on the hard work of others. We are all dwarves standing on the shoulders of giants.

Let us begin with positives. I wholly subscribe to McConachie's plea for a partnership between the arts and sciences 'where both sides can benefit from each other's knowledge', and Sutton and Tribble's plea to 'improve the language use on both sides of the academic split'.[47] Equally sound is the aim of mending the splits (inner/outer, mind/body, feeling/knowing) within the actor's body, and thereby developing a more accurate image of themselves in action. Finally, I think we would all be wise to follow the caution advised by Sutton and Tribble, particularly in our uses and even definitions of the cognitive sciences and (their place within) the field of neuroscience. They are not fixed intellectual edifices but fields that teem with contending opinions and definitions, where even the existence of such basic structures as mirror neurons is contested. Rather than carrying over objective and fixed meanings of science into the fuzzy field of the arts, I am more interested in establishing a dialogue consisting of questions of science and art. As I mentioned in the Preface, John Rothwell's habitual answer to my questions is 'I don't know, indeed, I don't know *how* we would know that.' We have spent nine years puzzling as to how we might know something about theatre practice using the ever-developing field of neurophysiology.

I am unsure about some of the claims made in the name of cognitive science. Take for example a historical overview offered by Kemp who sees in most interesting developments of theatre-thinking a foreshadowing of cognitive science. Diderot's 'analysis was prescient when viewed in the context of cognitive science'.[48] François Delsarte's 'intuitive recognition of the connections between thought, emotion, and behaviour anticipates many of the findings of cognitive science'.[49] Statements by Stanislavsky on the relation between physical action and psychological truth 'demonstrated an intuitive prescience of what cognitive science now tells us about the relationship between physical action, thought, and feelings'.[50] Continuing his historical survey he claims that Grotowski's belief in a *via negativa* 'anticipates the

---

[47]Sutton and Tribble 2013: 83.
[48]Kemp 2012: 2.
[49]Kemp 2012: 4.
[50]Kemp 2012: 6.

current cognitive understanding of interpersonal communication as a synthesis of unconscious biological impulses and conscious thought'[51] and that Jacques Lecoq's ideas also bear 'an extraordinary synchrony with the discoveries of cognitive science'.[52] By claiming that cognitive science has foreshadowed most major shifts in theatrical practice from Diderot to Lecoq, Kemp risks stating that by being everything it is therefore nothing in particular.

Blair argues that the objectivity of the cognitive approach lies in the fact that it is based on 'the general process by which all human beings work' rather than relying on the actor's individual 'psyche'.[53] But do all human beings work in the same way? And how can the specific problems of an actor working in a particular genre of theatre be answered by processes that are typical of 'all human beings'? Of course we (i.e. the neurotypical majority) all share the same basic neural structures, but it needs to be argued carefully how a knowledge of these neural processes can illuminate questions and problems that are peculiar to theatre practice.

Concerning how we articulate our approach to understanding the actor's body, I completely agree that we need to be careful in our choice of language and terminology, a caveat that recalls Barba's warning above. However, I am not sure that the fuzzy thinking of theatre practice can be 'translated' into the more objective, precise and accurate language of cognitive or neuroscience. A form of expression is a way of thinking with its own underpinning assumptions. Rather than dispensing with the language of theatre practice I aim to understand what is meant by oppositions like inside-out and outside-in, terms like 'centre' and instructions like 'don't think, do' (i.e. the very expressions rejected by Blair and Lutterbie). I shall argue that even if we can't quite offer objective descriptions of theatre terms and processes, could we (both scientists and artists) at least accept that behind the term there is a thing or problem or question worth studying, even if it eludes the capability of neuroscience to explain it? Far from rejecting theatre terms I am interested in exploring their possible meaning.

My broader concerns about choosing cognitive science as a methodological model for understanding theatre practice are well articulated by neuroscientist Joseph Ledoux who argues, 'First of all, by its very definition, cognitive science is a science of only a part of the mind – the cognitive part – and not a science of the whole mind.'[54] He notes how it is 'now widely recognised that we can have conscious access to the outcome of cognitive processes, but we are not usually aware of the processes that were involved in generating that content. Our perceptions, memories, and thoughts generally work in happy ignorance of the processes that make them possible.'[55] Of

---

[51]Kemp 2012: 11.
[52]Kemp 2012: 12.
[53]Blair 2008: 4.
[54]Ledoux 2002: 24.
[55]Ledoux 2002: 23.

course cognitive scientists are aware that many cognitive processes do not take place in the conscious mind, but we theatre commentators need to take account of the extent and therefore importance of the non-conscious mind. Ledoux points to a main theme that runs through my book – that, in the oft-quoted words of Polyani, 'We know more than we can tell.' This is what he calls 'tacit knowledge'. The question of how we can understand a body whose operation is mostly invisible to conscious reflection will be asked in a number of different ways through my book. The other major and very basic omission in most of the writings of theatre commentators inspired by cognitive science was their lack of reference to nerves or nervous systems.

III Neurophysiology and Other Scientific Approaches

An Approach Where 'Interdisciplinary' Means 'Wide'

I shall begin with a plea from the Soviet neurologist Nikolai Bernstein (1896–1966) for a general rather than a narrow perspective on mental phenomena, because any narrowing 'deprives people of the irresistible beauty of wide general education […] it emasculates creative thinking, impoverishes their work with respect to fresh ideas and wide perspectives'.[56] The same could be said of how Moshe Feldenkrais approached education, drawing together his understanding of Judo, physics and structural engineering to create a Method whose underlying thinking was almost entirely hidden, leaving the student with a structured procedure through which they could make their own discoveries.

We have already seen McConachie propose a partnership between 'scientists and scholars in the arts, where both sides can benefit from each other's knowledge'[57] and Berthoz argue that scientists have much to learn about the body from sculptors and dancers. Mark Johnson adds his voice by placing the arts within a broader realm of enquiry. In the preface to *The Meaning of the Body* (2007) he lists a number of harmful misconceptions that can impede our understanding of the human body, chief amongst which are that '1) the mind is disembodied, 2) thinking transcends feeling, 3) feelings are not part of meaning and knowledge, 4) aesthetics concerns matters of mere subjective taste, and 5) the arts are a luxury (rather than being conditions of full human flourishing).'[58] Such an affirmation of the arts makes the argument as to why scientists and artists should try to work together. As Amy Cook pointed out above, there is no monumental edifice called

---

[56]Bernstein 1996: 5.
[57]McConachie 2008: 16.
[58]Johnson 2007: xi.

'cognitive science' or neuroscience, for that matter: both are parts of a vast field in which countless types of research take place.

In his *How the Body Shapes the Mind* (2005) Shaun Gallagher explains the non-conscious processes that shape human experience in terms of this interdisciplinarity. He argues they can be grasped 'neither through phenomenology alone, nor through neuroscientific studies alone, nor through cognitive and behavioural approaches alone'. The only way is through a 'combined deployment of all these disciplines' and then one can 'outline a picture of embodied cognition that is rich and demanding of further investigation'.[59] Andy Clark echoes this necessary interdisciplinarity in *Supersizing the Mind* (2011). His approach is 'an unusual mix of neuroscience, computational, dynamical, and information theoretic understandings, "brute" physiology, ecological sensitivity, and attention to the stacked designer cocoons in which we grow, work, think, and act'.[60] When discussing audience response (2008) McConachie describes a similar interdisciplinary mix of 'cognitive neuroscientists, psychologists, philosophers, evolutionary theorists, and linguists' all of whom 'disagree about many aspects of consciousness, emotions, spatial perception, speech, and all of the other processes and attributes that facilitate performance spectatorship'.[61] Many of the books on which I have drawn upon for this study take a multi-disciplinary approach to their understanding of the human body in action.

In explaining his book *The Emotional Brain* (1996) neurologist Joseph Ledoux echoes Barba when he states that it is 'not about mapping one area of knowledge (the psychology of emotion) onto another (brain function). It is instead about how studies of brain function allow us to understand emotion as a psychological process in new ways.'[62] How an actor elicits emotion on stage is a hugely contested question that can possibly be opened out by such 'new ways' as suggested by Ledoux. Ultimately, we are all trying to make sense of something that we all recognize as a 'thing' even if we come at it from different perspectives and use different methods of analysis and description to understand it. Ledoux points out that his study is a corrective to cognitive science which has long ignored the study of emotion, and indeed 'treats minds like computers and has traditionally been more interested in how people and machines solve logical problems or play chess than in why we are sometimes happy and sometimes sad.'[63] While this certainly doesn't reflect the contemporary field of cognitive science it introduces an important theme in my book: we cannot treat humans like machines. An opposition that is rarely made (Bernstein being a notable exception) is that between the living organism and the machine, one which will resonate throughout this study, whether it be in a

---

[59]Gallagher 2005: 133.
[60]Clark 2011: 219.
[61]McConachie 2008: 6.
[62]Ledoux 1998: 23.
[63]Ledoux 1998: 20.

discussion of Meyerhold's Biomechanics (in Chapter 8), or Scott Kelso's Dynamic Patterns. What follows is a resumé of some of the key ideas and terms that I shall be using throughout this book.

Systems Theory and Dynamic Patterns

In his extraordinary *The Ecological Approach to Visual Perception* (1986) James Gibson argues, 'What psychology needs is the kind of thinking that is beginning to be attempted in what is loosely called systems theory.'[64] There are several characteristics of systems theory and these centre upon the relationship between the constituent parts of a given system: firstly, that their sum can be greater when it expresses emergent behaviour, and secondly that a change in one part can result in a change of the whole. By drawing on this theory one can begin to understand 'holism' as a dynamic process. This system does not operate according to a pre-installed programme but is capable of adapting to its environment and of learning from these interactions and adaptations. This kind of self-organizing system is necessary once one has dispensed with the dualist idea of a little person in your head who directs the movements of your body. An example of this theory in action can be found in Lutterbie's *General Theory of Acting* (2001), which draws on Scott Kelso's *Dynamics Patterns* (1995) to explain the work of the actor.

Loops and Re-Entry

Few theatre scholars make reference to the crucial opposition between dynamic and static analysis. Static analysis relies on fixed correspondences between structure and function. An example would be Franz Gall's (1758–1828) Phrenology where bumps in the skull are taken to correspond to emotional and intellectual faculties: thus Area 5 corresponds to 'combativeness', while Area 6 corresponds to 'destructiveness' (this is discussed more fully in Chapter 3). Over a century later Korbinian Brodmann (1868–1918) created a mapping of the neocortex where Area 5 is the Somatosensory Association Cortex and Area 6 the Premotor Cortex and Supplementary Motor Cortex. Common to these very different approaches is the notion that specific functions correspond to particular parts of the brain in an unchanging relationship.

A dynamic approach considers mental processes as time-based processes occurring between multiple sites in the brain, sometimes simultaneously, and thus cannot be represented as a snapshot, that is, as a fixed image. These are processes that occur across space (different parts of the brain) *and* time (that is usually measured in thousandths of a second). In Edelman and Tononi's

---

[64]Gibson 1986: 2.

A Universe of Consciousness (2000) they argue that a given function (an emotion or a perception) corresponds to a rhythmic pattern in which different parts of the brain are simultaneously activated, and messages are sent forward and back between them. They call this 're-entry' which they define as 'the ongoing, recursive interchange of parallel signals between reciprocally connected areas of the brain, an interchange that continually coordinates the activities of these areas' maps to each other in space and time'.[65] Although I am trying to avoid long quotations involving technical terms, the following is important as it brings together many themes discussed thus far.

> This synchronous firing of widely dispersed neurons that are connected by re-entry is the basis for the integration of perceptual and motor processes. Re-entry allows for a unity of perception and behaviour that would otherwise be impossible, given the absence in the brain of a unique, computer-like central processor with detailed instructions or of algorithmic calculations for the coordination of functionally segregated areas. Indeed, if we were asked to go beyond what is merely special and name the *unique* feature of higher brains, we would say it is re-entry.[66]

The first point is that re-entry accounts for how perceptual (or sensory) and motor processes are integrated. In any activity there is a constant recursive (to and fro) looping between our sensing and our moving; this union of 'perception and behaviour' is the very basis of intelligent movement. (Once again we see a challenge to any simplified account of the relation between sensory and motor nerves.) The second point brings us back to what happens in the absence of a 'unique, computer-like central processor'. Rather than a machine we are an exquisitely self-organized organic system that makes sense by means of fabulously complex patterns of connection between different parts of the brain. Forget maps and think of events happening in both space and time; maybe one could call it an orchestral process. It is a process that accounts for how we are constantly learning, and in and through that process changing the structure of our brains.

The Extended Brain

In *Supersizing the Brain* Andy Clark explains how functions that we think of happening within the brain are actually a result of a similarly recursive to and fro movement between brain, body and external environment. His image of the human organism involves what he calls 'the extraorganismic environment' (i.e. the

---

[65] Edelman and Tononi 2000: 48.
[66] Edelman and Tononi 2000: 49.

world outside the bodily organism). He calls this the extended model according to which 'certain forms of human cognising include inextricable tangles of feedback, feed-forward, and feed-around loops: loops that promiscuously criss-cross the boundaries of brain, body, and world'.[67] Once again, we are dealing with complex looping patterns rather than simpler linear progression: knots and tangles rather than straight lines.

What I admire so much about many of the scientists I have studied is the creativity with which they devise their experiments. To explore the nature of the extended mind Clark asked subjects to follow the computer game Tetris which involves shifting different coloured blocks from one area of the screen to another. While playing the game the subjects' eye movements were recorded, and Clark thereby discovered that rather than making a mental plan (or inner representation) to solve the spatial problem, they constantly referred back to the screen just before making a move. His theory that we operate 'just in time' has great application to acting, and could explain the capacity to be ready and available (as I shall demonstrate at the end of this book). Thus 'sensing is used repeatedly, with the external scene functioning as an information store to be called upon just in time for the task fragment at hand'. He stresses the importance of the fact that sensing 'acts as a constantly available channel that productively couples agent and environment' rather than converting these external signals 'into a persisting inner model of the external scene'.[68]

Clark's argument is a detailed critique of the 'outside-in' model of perception and action where the senses are used 'to get enough information inside, past the visual bottleneck, so as to allow the resonating system to "throw away the world" and solve the problem wholly internally'. Clark instead argues for a constant engagement with the world whereby 'they use the sensor as *an open conduit allowing environmental magnitudes to exert a constant influence on behaviour*'.[69] Putting the question more generally, does problem-solving happen inside a head that is furnished with information from external sensors, or is it a constant negotiation with the external environment? Is it the search for an internally represented picture or algorithm (a static solution), or is it an ongoing dynamic process? I hope that the application to theatre practice is already evident: this is a paradigm example of getting out of your head and, through your body, into the space and activity around you. I would argue that there is no exercise in *Training the Actor's Body* that does not involve this sensory-cognitive engagement with the studio environment.

---

[67]Clark 2011: xxviii.
[68]Clark 2011: 15.
[69]Clark 2011: 16.

How the Body Becomes Absent

Clark offers another example of the extended brain, this time a physical one. He gives the example of how, through regular use, a blind person's stick can become an extension of themselves: the point of connection – Clark calls it 'the point of critical (heuristic) interface' – moves from the hand on the stick, to the end of the stick with the solid objects it touches. Through practice the 'it' becomes 'I' as 'the new agent-tool interface itself fades from view, and the proper picture is one of an extended or enhanced agent confronting the (wider) world'.[70] Clark's examples of how we extend ourselves into space through heuristic activity – the scanning process in the puzzle, the integration of a stick in the touching of a stick – introduces another major theme that will run through my argument. This concerns actor training being a heuristic approach (heuristic coming from the ancient Greek verb, *Euriskein,* to find out).[71] When the stick becomes an extension of myself it ceases to be an external instrument and thus becomes absent in my perception: my attention is now on the world revealed by the the movements I make with my stick. This is the subject of Drew Leder's *The Absent Body* (1990), a poetic meditation upon this process whereby the body in its investigation of the world, or in action, becomes invisible. Much training follows a process whereby skilful activity first has to be guided through conscious thought and attention, but as the skill becomes mastered so it will be performed without such attention; after practice one can do it 'with one's eyes closed' or 'in one's sleep'. This revisits two themes already identified in the Introduction: firstly about how we consider our body as an instrument and secondly that when it does become so, at the same moment it becomes invisible, a transparent means of achieving a task.

Arnold describes the same process of erasure when a sportsperson has mastered a particular skill: 'when I am caught up in an on-going performative project, although my bodily powers are being utilised, I not think of them as a means towards an end. Rather in the absorbed "heres" and "nows" of the action my ensemble of powers are experienced as that which I am.'[72] In this sense the skill or technique has become 'tacit' (i.e. 'unspoken') knowledge. The skill becomes an acquired habit, an activity we perform without thinking about it. This net of themes – heuristic activity, the absent body, tacit knowledge, habit – will weave throughout my book.

---

[70]Clark 2011: 31.
[71]Section 3 of Chapter 2 in my *Training the Actor's Body* (2016) deals with heuristic training.
[72]Arnold 1979: 3.

The Intelligence of Physical Skill and Action

In his book *Intelligence in the Flesh,* Guy Claxton explains that tacit knowledge is hard to define because it 'is such a fine web of contingent possibilities, built up through years of experience, that it simply cannot be rendered down into words. The neurochemical loops and networks that underpin your expertise are orders of magnitude more intricate than any vocabulary, however technical, could hope to capture.'[73] Claxton mischievously quoted a teacher of education who said: 'If you can explain it, you don't *really* understand it.'[74]

My book on actor training (2018) addressed the problem of how and what actors learn. In this book I am interested in how we understand the body that does the learning, and the 'body' that results from this learning. My study could be classed as what Claxton calls a New Materialism where we are interested in 'the quiet, protracted hands-on pleasures of making, mending, customising and perfecting physical skills'.[75] I will follow Claxton's lead in thinking that 'we're fundamentally built for action, not for thinking or understanding, and that, as a consequence, our intelligence is deeply orientated towards the construction of effective and appropriate behaviour'.[76] He goes on to argue that this 'practical, embodied intelligence is the deepest, oldest, most fundamental and most important intelligence of the lot; and the others are aspects or outgrowths of this basic, bodily capability'.[77]

At the beginning of their book Edelman and Tononi ask, 'How can our understanding of consciousness help connect strictly scientific descriptions to the wider domain of human knowledge and experience?'[78] In writing this book I aim to connect with 'the wider domain of human knowledge and experience', the domain to which writers like Claxton, Ingold and Johnson have all made such significant and illuminating contributions.

Summary of Main Points

This is a chapter mostly of questions and problems rather than answers. We began with Peter Arnold asking how it is that we know ourselves. Through our experience of our bodily selves, he answers. Neuroscientists Edelman and Tononi point to their dilemma as scientists whose subject matter is consciousness: how can they take the objective stance of scientific when consciousness is what makes me *me*?

---

[73]Claxton 2015: 232.
[74]Claxton 2015: 233.
[75]Claxton 2015: 9.
[76]Claxton 2015: 5.
[77]Claxton 2015: 9.
[78]Edelman and Tononi 2000: xii.

The next problem lies in the nature of our object of study, the body. How does one study an organism that is in constant motion and change? The answer is by taking a systems approach that rejects simple linear relations between things and events. Linear relations assume a fixed geometrical space, whereas we will be dealing with events that demand us thinking of the fourth dimension of time. Meaning can no longer be captured as snapshots but rather as time-based processes. We will take a dynamic rather than a static approach in this book.

This chapter, indeed this book, rests on the unsettling and exploration of various distinctions and oppositions: mind and body, disembodied/embodied, science and art, moving and sensing, sensing and thinking. A figure that lies behind many of these oppositions is that between inner and outer.

A group of important theatre commentator/practitioners demonstrate how cognitive science can offer a new way of understanding performance. Part of this claim rests on the belief that a more objective, evidence-based approach will replace the fuzzy thinking of theatre practitioners. I shall propose a broader approach that includes writers from across a number of fields, including sociology, philosophy and ecological psychology. This book will take that very fuzzy thinking and examine its potential to generate a very specific set of problems for sciences of the brain and body. This discussion introduced another opposition, that between conscious and unconscious. How does one discuss processes which mostly take place beneath the threshold of consciousness? This explains Polyani's famous statement 'We know more than we can tell' and why he calls this tacit knowledge.

Clark brings two of these oppositions together when he argues that not all thinking takes place inside the head, but in the outside world, and therefore unsettles the distinction between perception and cognition. In his analysis of how we play Tetris he demonstrates how sensing (visual perception in the environment) is intimately to cognition. He also introduces the strange dialectic between absence and presence when he examines how we render instruments invisible in our very use of them as means of perception. The body extends into the world, destroying the idea of them being separated by the envelope of the skin.

2 TRAINING: FROM THE EVERYDAY BODY TO THE ACTOR'S BODY

Introduction

The distinction between these two 'bodies' is, as I have already pointed out, a necessary device for the purposes of my argument. Given that we are dealing with one and the same body much of my argument in this book rests on the contention that one way of rethinking the actor's body is by considering recent research into the physiology of the human body.

In reality, we are dealing with a person's body that is transformed over time through training and practice. We can judge the outcome of that training by comparing the state and capacity of this body before and after. This chapter will deal with questions of how we learn, which in turn involves questions of training and memory, and how we access or act upon this learning. My interest lies in the learning of skills and techniques, that is, the field of knowing how, rather than knowing what (returning to Ryle's distinction). Much of my argument rests on the contention that the actor has to know the capacity of their given body before it can become a creative resource for them; they need to know what they are working with. This is easier said than done since in our everyday attitude we take our bodies for granted. We are not aware of them unless we become injured or ill.

In the case of learning 'know how' we are dealing with knowledge that is embodied. We therefore need to recognize that the body-before-training is not some blank sheet, but a person who has already learned a variety of fundamental movement skills from crawling to standing, walking to jumping. Most of these seemingly unremarkable skills were self-taught through a process of trial and error, driven by the desire to find out about the world and act autonomously (returning us to the heuristic spirit discussed in Chapter 1[1]). As a result, these skills have an indelibly personal inflection: our way of walking is as recognizable as our handwriting. Our

---

[1]McCaw 2018: 41–2 (Section 2.3 A heuristic approach to training), 239.

personal repertoire of skills constitutes 'our' way of doing things. And yet while our friends might easily recognize how we walk, our way of walking is invisible to us. Both our bodies and our way of using them are pretty much invisible to us. This lends another dimension to Polyani's saying, 'We know more that we can tell'. Put another way, we can do things but cannot explain how we do them. This makes re-training difficult. In order to negotiate the transition from a given to a created/creative body, the actor has to become aware of a set of deeply embedded skills which have been taken for granted. Training is already an act of rethinking the body.

Stanislavsky recognized the constant negotiation that needs to take place between the actor and their given body. He observes, 'It would seem that the theatre requires us to re-learn, re-understand, re-experience things we know in life onstage in a public show'.[2] This explains 'why we have to learn to walk, move, sit, lie down all over again', later adding, 'you must learn to look and see, listen and hear onstage, too'.[3] Stanislavsky is arguing that while an actor may know how to sit, stand, look and listen in everyday life, when asked to do this on stage, in front of an audience, these 'natural' skills desert them. He goes further by demanding that this process of training (and reflection) should continue throughout an actor's career, both for personal and physiological reasons. Every 'exacting actor, however great, at certain intervals, say every four or five years, must go back and study anew. It is also necessary for him periodically to place his voice – it changes with time'. Stanislavsky then adds another reason for such periods of reflective training: 'He must also rid himself of those habits which have adhered to him like dirt' and concludes with the demand: 'Do not think of performance – think only of training, training, training'.[4]

Stanislavsky's insistence on lifelong training touches on another paradox of actor training. When engaged in training an actor has to think through many aspects of technique consciously. But this technique becomes effective only when it can be performed *without thinking*; that is, our bodies become effective 'instruments' only once they have become invisible. This returns us to the discussion about tacit knowledge which we began in Chapter 1. According to Stanislavsky, while practical knowledge – or call it technique – has to be acquired consciously it can only be effectively performed unconsciously, and because it is being performed unconsciously the actor has therefore to periodically review their technique. To better understand this paradox let us examine what this technique consists of.

What is it that the actor does with their body? In the realist tradition an actor takes on how they have seen and heard other people move and speak, thus creating a way of doing and speaking that approximates to a given character. In *Training the Actor's Body* I suggested that a character is a unique way of moving and doing in the world (just as everyone has their unique way of moving). As I have argued in

---

[2]Stanislavsky 2008b: 601.
[3]Stanislavsky 2008b: 93.
[4]Toporkov 1999: 155.

that book, an understanding of movement is central to actor training. One aim of that training is to develop a kind of movement intelligence, a sensitivity to all the shades and colours of moving.

The gist of what I want to say about sensitivity is captured in this quotation from Gibson:

> The question then is, how do the senses work? Since the senses are being considered as perceptual systems, the question is not how the receptors work, or how the nerve cells work, or where the impulses go, but how the systems work as a whole. We are interested in the useful sense, the organs by which an organism can take account of its environment and cope with objective facts.[5]

I shall follow Gibson's lead and study how the actor's body works 'as a whole', more particularly, how an actor makes sense from and with its senses, rather than examining the specific functions of organs. This explains why I am taking a physiological rather than an anatomical approach to the body: physiology 'deals with the normal functioning of living organisms and their systems and organs' (OED). My interest is not in the body on the dissection table, but the living body in action.

All this to say that training is what provides the bridge between the everyday and the actor's body. This training has to be lifelong precisely because of the nature of embodied learning. A sign that a skill has been fully learned is that it becomes invisible (we can do it with our eyes shut, in our sleep, etc.). After a time this invisibly performed skill may need attention (owing to changes in the body or the development of bad habits) and thus it has to become visible again. The cycle of continuous learning is: conscious learning to unconscious performance back to conscious re-learning.

A great part of this training concerns developing a sensitivity to how we move. Neurophysiology can help us understand the means by which an actor becomes more sensitive to their own way of moving as well as the movement styles of others. At the heart of this is the connection between sensing and moving.

Many neuroscientists suggest that movement is the reason we have a brain in the first place. In the first section of this chapter I want to understand the roots of our movement through tracing its evolution from the simplest moving beings – ticks, sea squirts and sea snails – up to the most complex, humans. By means of this seeming detour I hope to identify how the movement of the least sophisticated creatures is, like our own, guided by an exquisite interrelation between motor and sensory nervous systems. At the apex of this interrelation is the recently discovered mirror neuron, which has both a sensory and motor function.

A connection between sense and movement is necessary because we exist in an environment which demands choices of action from us. Our movement is a

---

[5]Gibson 1968: 6.

response to the internal and external environment. No surprise that Stanislavsky would write about the actor having to grasp the 'given circumstances' of a character. Pushing this interrelation of sensory and nervous systems further I shall argue that our bodies are not set off from the world, but are part of it (returning us to Andy Clark's notion of the 'extended body' discussed in Chapter 1). I shall finish with three brief studies of the moving body which further explore the relation between moving and feeling. Hopefully, by examining some of the most fundamental aspects of moving and being this chapter will help us rethink the actor's body.

Some parts of this chapter may seem to be very far from questions of actor-training: how is a study of the worlds of the tick or the sea-squirt going to illuminate our understanding of the actor's body? I have already argued that the human organism is fiendishly complex. To understand some basic behaviours of living organisms it is easier to study simpler structures. This also makes the equally important point that the sensory-motor connections that establish a meaningful relation between self and environment are basic to all living things. Ticks and humans both need to know when to act, both being subject to the same laws of survival and reproduction in their given worlds. These parables of the tick, sea-squirt and sea-snail are all told with the ultimate aim of better understanding how an actor can become more sensitive to the stage environment, and to the objects and other people found within it.

I Why Do We Have a Brain?

Action Takes Place within the Given Circumstances of an Environment

In *A Foray into the World of Animals and Humans* (2010/1934), Jakob von Uexküll explores how animals create meaning through their interaction with their surrounding environment. His argument is that body, world and meaning come together through an animal's purposeful action. 'We begin, therefore, with a subject located in its environment and research its harmonious relationships to the individual objects that present themselves to the subject as carriers of meaning.'[6] He later explains that nothing is left to chance in nature, but 'that the animal and its medium are everywhere connected by an intimate meaning rule which binds the two in a duet in which the properties of both partners are composed contrapuntally to one another'.[7] Here we are dealing with what one might call an ecological theory of human meaning, rooted in action that will later be articulated by writers like Gibson, Ingold, Claxton and Sennett.

---

[6]Uexküll 2010: 172.
[7]Uexküll 2010: 174.

Writing from the perspective of theatre practice Blair grasps the importance of this ecological conception of action: 'We cannot locate meaning in the text, life in the cell, the person in the body, knowledge in the brain, a memory in a neuron. Rather, these are all active, dynamic processes, existing only in interactive behaviours of cultural, social, biological and physical environment systems.'[8] Once again, we return to a defence of an approach that deals with the whole body acting in a multi-levelled environment. We have to appreciate that an actor on stage operates at a multisensory and multi-behavioural level.

The intelligence of animals and humans alike lies in judging how, where, when (and with whom) an action should be taken. Time is the quickening element in processes that happen within organisms and, in a similar way, the timing of real-world action is crucial: too early or too late may result in the failure or partial success of the action. Berthoz argues that action is not movement but 'the intention to interact with the world or with oneself as part of the world. Action always has a goal; it is always backed up by purpose. It thus becomes the organizer of perception, the organizer of the perceived world.'[9] Note how Berthoz links perception and action, thus underlining the important connection of the sensory and the motor nervous systems. The bigger point is his distinction between movement (a mechanical fact) and action (a movement invested with meaning). One of my favourite teachers, Dominique Dupuy, would scream 'faire un acte!' (make an act) to encourage his students to invest their movements with meaning. (Geraldine Stephenson often used to exclaim, 'Your hands are meaningless today!')

Just as action is at the heart of meaning in the living world, so it is in theatre. Stanislavsky argues, 'Acting is action. *The basis of theatre is doing, dynamism.* The word "drama" itself in Ancient Greek means, "an action being performed."' (The Greek word is δρᾶν (*dran*) meaning to do, act, or perform.) The passage continues: 'So, drama is an action we can see being performed, and, when he comes on, the actor becomes an agent in that action.'[10] This, of course, is not the same action as that being described by the non-theatrical writers above. Here we are dealing with 'an action being performed': actions that have been rehearsed and then repeatedly performed. In 1995 Peter Brook created a piece exploring systems of rehearsal and based it on *Hamlet*, the title *Qui est la*? being the first line of the play (Bernado's 'Who's there?'). No surprise he chose a play that centred on decisions and dilemmas about when to act and questions of acting in theatre. Brook played on the ambiguity of the question, 'When to act?' since it has completely different meanings in the contexts of philosophy and theatre, a difference that extends to how we understand the body, space and time in these two very different contexts. To explore this double meaning further let us turn to the notion of 'being in the

---

[8]Blair in Shaughnessy 2013: 140.
[9]Berthoz 2003: xi.
[10]Stanislavsky 2008b: 40.

moment'. This is the moment of taking action. Below we shall see how the notion of a 'moment' is understood in the natural world.

In his account of the world of the blood-sucking tick Uexküll offers a vivid answer to the question 'When to act?' Equipped only with a sense of smell and touch, the tick spends much of its life on the branch of a bush or tree waiting for the scent of a passing animal to prompt it into action. After detecting the scent the tick will then drop onto the beast and be guided through the fur by the sense of increasing warmth until it reaches the skin where it will start to suck the animal's blood. A tick can survive for eighteen years without eating until the critical moment arrives when it is stirred into action by the scent of a passing animal. Uexküll reflects on the experience of time as constituted by a 'moment' which he defines as 'the shortest segment of time in which the world exhibits no changes. For a moment's duration, the world stands still.' In the world of the tick a moment can last up to eighteen years as compared to the human's which 'lasts one eighteenth of a second'.[11] A moment is a unit of time experienced rather than a duration measured. The scale may be incommensurate – humans can experience 567 million moments for the tick's one – but both embody the principle that meaning is related to the moment of action.

We take action for a reason, most often as a result of an environmental cue, something which has meaning to us. The tick's sense of smell is acutely attuned to the scent of butyric acid (i.e. the smell of blood). Their sensors are geared to what they need to sense and are thus tailored (one could just as easily say 'limited') to their existential needs. Their sense of their surroundings is as different to ours as is their sense of time. The tick makes sense of its world thanks to two sets of cells, the 'perception cells' responding to 'external groups of stimuli, which present themselves to the animal subject in the form of questions' and 'effect cells' which control 'the movement of the effectors, which impart the animal subject's answers to the outside world'.[12] (Which should remind us of Berthoz's connection between perception and action, and which in turn connects with an actor's responsiveness on stage.)

An exploration of two slightly more sophisticated organisms will develop this notion of ecological action and explain why we have brains. The first is the sea-squirt which is remarkable because in its larval state it has a basic brain, but once attached to a rock and having achieved its adult form it then consumes this protein-rich organ. This surely prompts the question: why did it need a brain in the first place? Basically, because the larva moves intentionally and the sea-squirt doesn't. To achieve its task of finding the rock or surface where the water currents are

---

[11]Uexküll 2010: 52.
[12]Uexküll 2010: 47.

nutrient-rich the larva needs motor nerves to move, sensory nerves to guide those movements and other sensory receptors to provide information about its ideal environment. The tick and the sea-squirt larva both demonstrate this necessary relationship between movement and sensation (action informed by perception), and the symbiotic relationship between the nature of a body and its environment. The body of a larval sea-squirt and of a tick are the way they are because of how they live in their environment.

In *The Development of Dexterity* (written in the 1940s, published and translated in 1996) Nikolai Bernstein offers a similar account of the cell specialization to Uexküll. Once again we are dealing with the development of a sensorimotor system by which motor cells are guided by sensory cells. Cells on 'the body surface, accommodate the carrying out of the jobs of *excitability* and *sensitivity;* others, deep in the body, learn to change shapes, to *contract,* and to provide *primitive movements'.*[13] He calls the first cells *receptive,* the second *contractile,* and argues that organisms that make a connection between them have 'a very serious, even decisive, biological advantage'. He points out that older organisms which lacked this connection between receptive and contractile cells could only move in 'ways that could frequently be senseless or even harmful'; however, newer organisms with a more sophisticated nervous system 'could *react* to external stimuli (for example, they could move directly to a potential prey or move away from a potential danger)'.[14] This is a very basic example of what I have been calling movement intelligence.

Eric Kandel offers a more detailed account of how sensory *neurons,* 'which are located in the skin and in various sense organs, respond to a specific type of stimulus from the outside world – mechanical pressure, (touch), light (vision), sound waves (hearing), or specific chemicals (smell and taste) – and send this information to the brain'. This is the sensory input. In turn, motor neurons 'send their axons out of the brain stem and spinal cord to effector cells, such as muscles',[15] which constitutes the motor output, or response. Think of how many exercises involve developing an actor's response to different sensory stimuli.

Bernstein's interest in this sensorimotor connection is twofold: it firstly allows the organism to make a motor response (or reaction) to an event in the environment, and secondly it allows the organism to make corrections to its own movement. The tick is completely stimulus-bound, having one reaction that is triggered by one stimulus. The *intelligence* of a more complex organism lies in its ability to make appropriate reactions and then monitor the effectiveness of these reactions.

---

[13]Bernstein 1996: 52.
[14]Bernstein 1996: 53.
[15]Kandel 2007: 66.

From Sensing to Learning

Thus far I have simply referred to there being a connection between moving and feeling. While the result of this connection is learning, we have not established how this connection is made. In his research on learning and memory, Eric Kandel defends his choice of studying very basic organisms. He argued that because, over the course of evolution, humans have retained 'some of the cellular mechanisms of learning and memory storage found in simpler animals'[16] it is possible to study 'the simplest instance of memory storage' in 'an animal with the simplest possible nervous system' and thereby the 'flow of information from sensory input to motor output'.[17] He therefore chose to explore how the sea slug *Aplysia* learns. He explains how the sea slug learns through sensory experience 'because it is essential for survival. An animal must learn to distinguish prey from predators, food that is nutritious from that which is poisonous, and a place to rest that is comfortable and safe from one that is crowded and dangerous'.[18] This may seem miles from performer training, but consider the experiment in its most general and basic terms: it concerns learning through the experience (the feeling) of doing. Memory (i.e. learning) also explains how an organism can begin to make intentional actions towards or away from things which favour or threaten survival.

How do sensory and motor nerves communicate with each other? Kandel calls this 'synaptic communication' between neurons and uses the image of one person whispering into another's ear.

> Thus, like lips whispering very close to an ear, synaptic communication between neurons has three basic components: the presynaptic terminal of the axon, which sends signals (corresponding to the lips in our analogy); the synaptic cleft (the space between lips and ear); and the postsynaptic site on the dendrite that receives signals (the ear).[19]

Synapse means 'junction' or 'connection' in ancient Greek, and this communication is the basis of learning and memory. Kandel discovered that in order to guarantee the strength and durability of this connection between an axon (which carries messages *from* the cell body) and a dendrite (which carries messages *to* the cell body), the cell body of the axon produces an extra synaptic terminal. In other words, a memory, a thing learned, consists of a physical alteration of the cell which means that the brain changes itself through its functional activity.

---

[16]Kandel 2007: 144.
[17]Kandel 2007: 143.
[18]Kandel 2007: 186.
[19]Kandel 2007: 65.

Kandel's experiments consisted of touching the skin of the *Aplysia* and noticing which kinds of repeated touching caused it to withdraw its vulnerable gills. The significance of this experiment lies in his demonstrating the difference between habituation and sensitisation. With repeated touching of the skin on its back the *Aplysia* became habituated to this non-threatening stimulus, which elicited no reaction once it had been recognized as familiar. However, touching the more vulnerable head or tail provoked an 'enhanced gill withdrawal reflex'.[20] Sensitization could be considered as the 'mirror image of habituation', since it develops 'a form of learned fear' which teaches the animal to 'attend and respond more vigorously to almost any stimulus after having been subjected to a threatening stimulus'.[21]

Through learning, an organism can make the energy-saving distinction between threatening and non-threatening stimuli, and thus past experience can inform future behaviour. Consider then the human animal which has hugely developed this faculty of self-correction, such that it can – say, in the practice of the Alexander Technique or Feldenkrais Method – detect a gap between stimulus and response, a gap in which the student can become aware of their habitual movement patterns, and thus learn how to change them. They learn how to recognize and avoid repeating the habitual response. It is precisely this kind of sensorimotor intelligence (or you could call it sensitivity) that any performer requires: you cannot change how you move if you don't know how you move in the first place. Feldenkrais spent much time helping students to recognize habits of action which had become 'invisible' through habit. Through developing an awareness of how we move, we can recognize and then (if we want) change our ways of acting and reacting. So much performer training is about getting rid of habits which stop you from doing what you want to do. All of which takes us back to Stanislavsky's demand that the actor relearn how to stand and sit.

There is also a transferable question that lies in the timing of the *Aplysia's* 'training'. Administering forty stimuli consecutively results in learning that lasts only a day whereas stimuli administered every day for four days produced learning that lasts for weeks. 'Spacing the training with periods of rest enhances the ability of an *Aplysia* to establish long-term memory.'[22] This experiment connects with both the Feldenkrais Method and performer training. Developing a sensitivity to movement takes time and cannot be achieved in one intensive session. The process of physical training (or rethinking our body) takes a long time. It is not simply a question of memorizing propositional knowledge, but of learning how to change one's way of moving according to these precepts and principles.

---

[20] Kandel 2007: 201.
[21] Kandel 2007: 169.
[22] Kandel 2007: 191–2.

Kandel offers a hint as to how the brain undertakes this process of learning. He argues that the brain has a built-in 'potential for many of an organism's behaviors' but that 'a creature's environment and learning alter the effectiveness of the pre-existing pathways, thereby leading to the expression of new patterns of behavior'.[23] Put less technically, learning is not so much the creation of completely new neural pathways, as much as altering the effectiveness of ones that already exist. This touches on two principles that are at the heart of the Feldenkrais Method and are central to my argument throughout this book. The first is that humans are wired (with 'pre-existing pathways') for learning. The second is that learning through experience, through feeling, leads to 'new patterns of behavior'. This ability to generate new patterns of behaviour contributes to the creativity and intelligence of the performer. Imagine a performer who mechanically repeated the same performance every night, or in rehearsal offered always the same response to a creative stimulus. They would be considered predictable and uncreative. Training is about (an actor or performer) developing an ever greater *range* of responses.

The examples discussed above offer a very simple model of sensory stimulus and motor response. What distinguishes the journey of humans is our adaptive genius: we are not structurally tied to any particular environment because we have developed the ability (for better or for worse) of creating our own environment. We are 'world open', to use the phrase of Berger and Luckmann,[24] because we have the imaginative capacity to overcome the potentially life-denying features of an environment and thereby make it inhabitable. Rather than being determined by our needs, we can reflect upon what we need and adapt the given environmental (natural and social) resources to satisfy those needs. An actor has the imaginative capacity to act *as if* in different environments, or as Stanislavsky would call them, *given circumstances*.

II Subjects and Objects in Space

Introduction

We shall need to reawaken our experience of the world as it appears to us in so far as we are in the world through our body, and in so far as we perceive the world with our body.[25]

Maurice Merleau-Ponty

---

[23]Kandel 2007: 202.
[24]Berger and Luckmann 1966.
[25]Merleau-Ponty 1962: 206.

Merleau-Ponty defines very precisely the argument of this section. He makes four points:

1 That we need to 'reawaken our experience of the world as it appears to us'.
2 That we are 'in the world through our body'.
3 That our experience of the world appears to us as it does precisely because of our body being 'in the world'.
4 The world appears to us thanks to the perceptual capacities of our bodies.

These points might seem uncontroversial but taken together they challenge common-sense notions about the relation between objects, the world and ourselves (as embodied subjects). One key notion is that there is a world consisting of objects whose existence is not contingent on our perception of them: their colour, scent and texture are considered inherent properties of the object, and are there for us as subjects to see, smell, touch.

What follows is a rethinking of the common-sense attitude towards living subjects and objects. Drawing on the research of a number of philosophers, biologists and psychologists I shall argue that living organisms adapt and respond to a specific environment which contains a specific range of objects that are vital to them. To make the point more clearly I shall return to simple organisms, and then scale up to the human animal. How is this relevant to work of the actor? I remember Simon McBurney talking to me about the 'world' of the play. Just as an animal's behaviour is a response to their given environment, so an actor's work is a response to the world of the play (this is an expanded version of Stanislavsky's given circumstances). When Claire Heggen asks her students to 'put themselves at the service of the object',[26] she is demanding this kind of creative response where the performer can be changed by their connection with objects or surroundings. So much of the actor's work (especially the actor-deviser) is about listening and attuning to whatever is in the stage environment: this might be nature of the props, lighting state, sound-design, pace of performance, audience feedback etc. As Merleau-Ponty observes, all of these are felt through the actor's body.

Objects, Action and Affordance in the World

An 'object' has meaning for an animal because it relates to their life, be it a source of food or of shelter, or a mortal threat. However, we should not think that object and subject are two separate things: Uexküll has already argued that the 'animal and its medium are everywhere connected by an intimate meaning rule which binds the two in a duet'.[27] An example of such a duet is the scent of butyric acid

---

[26]'Mettez-vous à la service de l'object' – from her 2003 DVD ROM.
[27]Uexküll 2010: 174.

and the tick's need for the blood of mammals. Humans are unaware of this scent because it is not part of our meaning-world.

Uexküll uses the German term *wirkraum* (translated as '*effect space*'[28]) to describe the space in which a subject and object are bound in this duet. The term 'effect space' connects with Uexküll's use of the term 'effector cells', that is, the neural cells that deal with action in the world. The German word *wirk* translates as 'real' and I would argue that each animal's reality is created by them through the effectual action they take as they go about their lives. If we take the principle that reality is about taking effective action, then we are not far from the world of theatre.

Uexküll goes on to describe the duet between the animal and its medium in greater detail when he notes how with the touch of our finger or the sweep of our eyes 'we confer a fine mosaic of place' upon the surface of an object. He describes this mosaic as 'a gift from the subject to things in its environment in visual as well as in tactile space, one which is not at all available in its surroundings'.[29] Put more simply, organisms confer meanings onto their surrounding medium; perceiving (e.g. seeing or touching) is thus a process of mapping onto objects what we already know of them. This challenges the common-sense account of things where the meanings of objects are already out there in the world, and that perception is simply a question of picking them up with our sensory organs. Now we turn to see how more recent thinkers have developed Uexküll's thinking about relations between subjects and objects.

In a book of similar imaginative breadth to Uexküll's, James Gibson's *An Environmental Approach to Visual Perception* (1979) introduces the term 'affordance' to describe this vital relation between an organism and its environment (what draws them into a duet). In Gibson's terms, the passing animal *affords* the tick the opportunity to feed: it is perceived because, and only because, it has existential value to the tick. Guy Claxton defines an affordance as 'a scene already parsed in terms of the things that I could possibly do. If we blend perceptions with our concerns, we might call these *opportunities*. An opportunity is an aspect of the world seen in the light of my current needs, interests or values'.[30] This is an example of enactive perception: we don't simply *see* a glass, we see something from which we can drink, a thing to be grasped and lifted. Although I am paraphrasing (and grossly simplifying) a whole field of research, the general point to be made is that perception is not a passive process of registering things in the world but an active and always ongoing process of meaning-making. Claxton is arguing that our perceptual set is geared to how we live and act in a given environment. Perception is a sense-making activity and is functionally connected with action.

---

[28]Uexküll 2010: 55.
[29]Uexküll 2010: 60–1.
[30]Claxton 2015: 71.

Uexküll described above how organisms map meaning on external objects. This is a stimulus-bound account of sensation and action which typifies a very simple living organism. The relation is an unchanging '=' sign where butyric acid = possible food source. Claxton develops Uexküll's model of perceptual mapping when he describes perception as 'a loop' which enables complex organisms like humans to be in a continual process of learning about the world.

> When we perceive something, we actually start on the inside: a prior belief, which is a model of the world in which there are objects in certain positions in space. Using this model, my brain can predict what signals my eyes and ears should be receiving. These predictions are compared with the actual signals, and, of course, there will be errors. My brain welcomes these errors. These errors teach my brain to perceive.[31]

In the context of a book about rethinking and training the body, 'These errors teach my brain to perceive' is a fantastically useful phrase. Claxton is just one of many voices[32] arguing against a simple outside/inside account of perception and action: the linear model of stimulus/response just doesn't account for the exquisite complexity of the way that we humans make sense of the world.

Andy Clark's notion of an Extended Mind could be seen as an extension of what Uexküll has called the *wirkraum*. Clark argues that thinking involves a constant perceptual engagement with the world, and thus could be considered to be partly taking place *in* the world and not inside the head. His 2011 book begins with an anecdote about how physicist Richard Feynman regards his workings on paper. The interviewer describes them as a record of the work going on in his head, and Feynman countered.

- I actually did the work on the paper, he said.

- Well, Weiner said, the work was done in your head, but the record is still here.

- No, it's not a record, not really. It's working. You have to work on paper and this is the paper. Okay?[33]

In other words, the pencilled workings are not a transcript of brain activity but his actual process of thinking. Clark argues, 'Feynman was actually *thinking* on the paper. The loop through pen and paper is part of the physical machinery

---

[31]Frith 2007: 126.

[32]Berthoz (2000, 2003) is one such voice, and he argues forcefully in his book with Petit (2008) for this model of feed-forward perception.

[33]In Clark 2011: xxv.

responsible for the shape of the flow of thoughts and ideas that we take, nonetheless, to be distinctively those of Richard Feynman.'[34]

In Chapter 1 of this book Clark demonstrated how gamers did not play the computer game *Tetris* by working out strategies in their heads, but through paying particular attention to what was happening on the screen. 'The idea is that the brain creates its programs so as to minimise the amount of working memory that is required and that eye motions are here recruited to place a new piece of information into memory.'[35] Feynman's sheet of paper and the computer screen are two examples of a *wirkraum,* a space on which one works out problems. I suggest that an actor's work takes place in the *wirkraum* of the stage or performance area: the creative thinking takes place in this meaning space, this space of action, this reality.

There is growing field of research that offers a very different account of the body's relation with the world outside it, one that demonstrates how simple binaries of 'inside/outside' are just too crude to be useful to a performer. Philosophers Lakoff and Johnson call this self-world relation 'embodied realism'[36] at the heart of which 'is our physical engagement with an environment in an ongoing series of interactions. There is a level of physical interaction in the world at which we have evolved to function very successfully, and an important part of our conceptual system is attuned to such functioning.'[37] Like so many of the non-theatre authors I have quoted, their argument is that sense-making results from this physical interaction with our external environment: meaning being rooted in bodily action and not mental cogitation. They continue that it is only a disembodied realism that 'creates an unbridgeable ontological chasm between "objects," which are "out there" and subjectivity which is "in here"' and conclude that 'as embodied, imaginative creatures, *we never were separate or divorced from reality in the first place*'.[38]

The Body's Orientation in the Environment

Merleau-Ponty stated above that we 'are in the world through our body'. Humans are uniquely oriented in the world being two-legged. We talk of our having a left and right, a front and back, top and bottom because we are vertically arrayed bodies with symmetrically organized limbs. If you had the body of an octopus your notion of left and right would mean nothing!

---

[34]Clark 2011: xxv.
[35]Clark 2011: 13.
[36]Chapter 6 of *Philosophy in the Flesh* (1999) is called 'Embodied Realism: Cognitive Science versus A Priori Philosophy'.
[37]Lakoff and Johnson 1999: 90.
[38]Lakoff and Johnson 1999: 93.

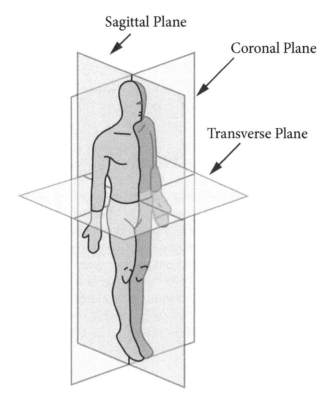

FIGURE 2.1 Three Planes of Movement.

This directional sense (i.e. left, right, up, down, front, back) is called an egocentric perception of space (literally, centred around the self). We can judge our sense of space through three planes of movement: for example, the median line runs down between the eyes, the filtrum, down to the navel and serves to separate left from right; the saggital line runs behind the ear, down through the hip and to the ankle separating front from back. The transverse line separating top from bottom is at the level of waist. (I shall analyse this spatial sense of our bodies in greater depth in Chapter 6.) A central contention of Lakoff and Johnson (1980, 1999) is that such fundamental aspects of orientation – which guide our every action – provide humans with the metaphorical basis for some of the key concepts by which we make sense of the world.

Claxton picks up on the theme of spatial orientation, noting that in addition to the egocentric attitude there is another way of understanding one's position in space. He begins by distinguishing between two types of action: in actions 'on the world, when we are close quarters. I might pinch it, unwrap it, kick it, play it, fight it, drink from it, type on it or paint it. For this type of action, my body is the origin, the *subject* so to speak, and action emanates from this centre, so I need an *egocentric* map'.[39] From this perspective, I see 'objects' out there with their meaning determined by the use I have for them. The second type of action 'enables me to move *through* the world so I can get where I want or need to be. In this frame, my body itself is an "object" that travels through space, so I need a map in which I can locate myself as one object amongst an array of others. This is called an *allocentric* map'.[40]

Mastering Objects in the World

Another way of understanding that objects aren't just out there in space for us to register is to follow a baby's developing ability to recognize objects as such. Our ability to make sense of the maelstrom of sensory data – which Feldman Barrett calls 'noisy information from our eyes, ears, nose and other organs'[41] – is a skill that is learned and perfected over time. In his book on cognitive development (1985) John Flavell explains just how long it takes a baby to master an understanding of objects 'out there'. He explains that establishing the 'object concept' is a six-stage process that ends with the child (aged 18–24 months) being able to conceive of 'an external entity that exists and may move about in complete independence of his own perceptual or motor contact with it'.[42] A child who has mastered the notion of object constancy will follow a toy with its eyes, and when it disappears behind a screen will predict when it will reappear from the other side: out of sight for this child is not out of mind. The child accepts that the object has a continuing existence even when it cannot be seen.

Flavell's explanation of how we learn to master the idea of objects having an existence in the world independent of ourselves leads onto a discussion of how we develop the ability to see people and ourselves from other points of view. This brings us back to the distinction between egocentric and allocentric perception. Claxton explains that as a child matures so it detaches itself from its 'default, egocentric constellation of habits and concerns, and see the world through other people's eyes'.[43] Such imaginary transposition allows them to play hide and seek better as they become able to imagine their playmates as the hunter, and thus predict their possible strategies. More generally, this faculty expands their social intelligence as they learn to see the world from different perspectives; it is also an ability to understanding how others see me: 'When I inhabit your vantage point,

---

[39]Claxton 2015: 94.
[40]Claxton 2015: 95.
[41]Feldman Barrett 2017: 27.
[42]Flavell 1985: 37.
[43]Claxton 2015: 216.

one of the things it enables me to see is myself. I can become an "object" to myself, with traits, temperament and habits as well as a visual appearance.'[44]

This faculty for transposition, for shifting vantage points and putting oneself in another person's shoes is surely a skill that every actor needs to develop. More generally, this allocentric sense of space is crucial for an actor (and anyone involved in field sports) to develop. Three exercises (47, 51, 57) in *Training the Actor's Body* directly address the development of an allocentric sense of space. I would also argue that sense is related is peripheral vision or what Zinder and I call 'soft focus'.

Flavell argues that mastering the out-thereness of objects could be 'the most important single acquisition in all of human cognitive growth',[45] but Claxton points to another equally important attitude towards the external world and that is 'an inquisitive inclination to mess about with the material we find, and get it to reveal additional affordances. If you fiddle with a stick you might reveal its ability to become a fishing rod. If you try smashing stones together, you might splinter off shards that can be found useful for cutting.'[46] While this brings us back to the theme of an intelligence rooted in doing, it also suggests an extension of Gibson's idea of affordance which I call 'creative affordance' where by 'messing about' an artist can *see* new uses for an everyday object. Picasso's *Bull's Head* (1942) is made from the saddle and handlebars of a bicycle. His genius lay in seeing a creative affordance in these mundane objects.

III What Does an Actor Need to Know about Human Physiology?

Introduction

It may seem eccentric that I have chosen to write about feet, muscles and skin. Surely I should have included hands. David McNeill has written a fascinating book (1992) on hands and how their gestures are inextricably linked to verbal communication which greatly informed Kemp's book on *Embodied Acting* (2012). As interesting as McNeill's study is, my argument lies in more general themes about the actor's body. We have to understand our feet because they bear our weight as we stand and walk; rather improbably, we balance our whole body on the very narrow platform of our feet. Gary Wragg, my tai chi instructor, argues that this martial art is about 'two big feet and a mind'. As for muscles, they are responsible for every move we make and every shape we assume. To focus on our skin is to challenge the notion of 'centred' body. Skin

---

[44]Claxton 2015: 217.
[45]Flavell 1985: 42.
[46]Claxton 2015: 202.

is our largest and most extensive sensory organ, a continuous surface that is in constant contact with the environment.

Feet

Since my focus is on the development of movement intelligence, and since this is fed by the information gleaned from sensation, I shall be sparing in anatomical detail. My approach is less about the naming and description of specific bones, muscles or nerves, and much more about their collective and interconnected function, that is, their physiology. Luke Dixon begins his book *Playacting* (2003) by introducing the foot, noting there are twenty-eight bones and describing the 'different kinds of bone'.

> The feet are for weight bearing and balance. Our entire body weight is borne by the base bones on each foot – these are the taluses. The talus spreads the weight, half back into the heel and half forward into the two sesamoids of metatarsal 1 and to metatarsals 2–5; so our big toe takes twice the weight of our other toes.[47]

Although this is useful in terms of understanding the distribution of weight, I am not sure the names of the bones will help me master my orientation and balance. After this basic account of the bones he assumes that the reader is 'aware of how the feet are constructed'.[48] Ten pages later, the reader is being instructed to 'Push against the floor. You know about your feet.'[49] Has the author really offered any grounds for the reader to know or find out more about their feet? How do we feel that pressure against the floor? How do we feel the connection between our feet and the rest of ourselves? Where Dixon offers a series of facts, a writer like Feldenkrais offers lessons where one can experience the action of these parts of our bodies. In Dixon's study the foot is isolated in terms of its connection through both the nervous system and our skeletal structure.

Ewan and Green take a much more experiential approach and write about how 'Footwork comes alive when the actor consciously acknowledges his past and present experiences of his feet: how they move him normally, how they move him through dance, sport, hiking, and so on.'[50] They then invite students to explore taking weight on different parts of the feet and to consider how this informs them about their own way of walking. It also means they know what to look for when observing someone else's walk. In other words, they have enabled a student to generate information about how they and by extension other people move. There are a number of stories about

---

[47]Dixon 2003: 6–7.
[48]Dixon 2003: 7.
[49]Dixon 2003: 16.
[50]Ewan and Green 2015: 19.

actors like Beryl Reid and Alec Guinness who begin their search for a character by looking for the right shoes. Their work on character begins with the way they walk. Ewan and Green add another dimension to footwork when they mention how 'Areas of the feet can be discovered through identification and naming: for example tai chi's bubbling well point; at the centre of the sole, and the use of the terms "ankle foot" and "heel foot" for the outside and inside sections of the feet.'[51]

Continuing the theme of 'Footwork', Tadashi Suzuki argues that actor training needs to start with the feet. Looking forward to the argument of Chapter 5 he argues that all 'physical techniques employed for the stage' involve learning how to control one's energy, centring it in the 'pelvic region'. It is precisely this skeletal connection between feet and pelvis that Dixon's analysis lacked. Suzuki considers his unique contribution to actor training is 'the idea of stamping the foot – forcing the development of a special consciousness based on this striking of the ground. This concept arises from my conviction that an actor's basic sense of his physicality comes from his feet.'[52] Stamping not only awakens the inner energy of the actor, but brings them into vital connection with the world: 'The feet alone can stamp and strike the earth, which represents man's unique foundation and authority. The feet have provided, up until now, the ultimate means of connection between man and earth.'[53] In these quotations we see Suzuki's poetic and philosophical plea for the actor to learn how to use feet and knees as a means of connection within him- or herself, with the ground beneath them, indeed with the universe. If we are to rethink the actor's body, then I would suggest we consider how this director/pedagogue offers an image of the body as a means of connection, through the skin on the soles of our feet, and the bones and joints of the lower leg.

Muscles

What facts about the musculature of the human body might help a student of theatre better understand their movement potential? The first and most basic fact is that a muscle can only do one thing: contract and then release that contraction. Lulu Sweigard (1974) focuses on the musculo-mechanical fact that because muscles are (mostly) attached to two bones, one bone needs to be stabilized so that the other is moved by the muscle contraction. Her lucid account of this complex process merits being quoted in full:

> Thus the performance of each pattern of movement is attended by a specific patterning of muscle action designed to control the position of the bones involved in that movement. This very complicated reflex action of stabilisation

---

[51]Ewan and Green 2015: 19.
[52]Suzuki 1992: 9.
[53]Suzuki 1992: 14–15.

is subject to continual change in the course of movement. The individual cannot direct it; his only influence is indirect concentration on the movement he wishes to perform.[54]

Later she continues: 'learning movement patterns requires concentration on the desired *effect* of muscle action and not on the muscle action itself, or any part of it.'[55] The conscious part of the brain focuses not upon the individual groups of muscles involved (the effectors), but rather on the desired outcome: lifting the glass, opening the door or whatever.

Our upright stance is the result of an even more complex relation between two sets of muscles. Feldenkrais explains this double action:

> The standing, or antigravity muscles are mostly extensors [...] i.e., those that open the articulations. The muscles of all articulations have their opposite numbers. While the articulation is being extended, the flexor that closes it is relaxing accordingly. This oscillatory flow of contraction from one muscle to its opposite number is called antagonism, and the muscles are said to be antagonistic.[56]

Feldenkrais spent much of his time pointing out to students that a good posture is one where neither sets of muscles (i.e. flexors and extensors) are overworking. If the flexor muscles around the stomach are always active, that means that the back muscles are over lengthened and cannot do their job properly. In *Body and Mature Behaviour* Feldenkrais notes that the cervical and lumbar curves in the spine are the result of muscle development in the baby, and their poor alignment can result in difficulties. The interplay between the cervical and lumbar parts of the spine is 'a unique part in the antigravity muscular adjustment. They may be considered a kind of sense organ.'[57] This leads to a fourth fact (more an image) about muscles: that all posture and body shape are a result of the action of muscles.

From Feldenkrais's explanation we can grasp that our upright posture is something that is created rather given. A skeleton is not a free-standing structure but requires the finely balanced interplay of muscles to keep it in tensile equilibrium. Think of a geodesic dome whose form and volume are maintained by the perfectly balanced tension between steel wires – a phenomenon known as tensegrity. The architect Buckminster Fuller borrowed the concept of tensegrity from sculptor Kenneth Snelson to demonstrate that the structural integrity of a structure can derive from the balanced tension between members rather than the compression struts, like pillars or support walls.

---

[54]Sweigard 1974: 144.
[55]Sweigard 1974: 145.
[56]Feldenkrais 2005: 54.
[57]Feldenkrais 2005: 101.

Grotowski writes very elegantly about a balance between building and relaxing muscles in his essay 'Exercises' (1979). He argues that on the one hand, actor training should not consist of weight training to develop muscle bulk since it only creates a 'brabançon', that is, a very stocky working horse used for ploughing. On the other hand, he warns against a certain practice of yoga which focuses purely on relaxation which results in 'a sort of atrophy or asthenia of the body'.[58] Asthenia is characterized by a floppiness, lack of energy and debility. Instead, he wants the agility and alertness of a cat, which even when at rest can pounce the moment it sees a mouse. There is a certain state of muscular tensegrity that the actor, like the cat, needs to develop. In this optimal tensegrity lies the actor's readiness to move.

If tensegrity is an image of a perfectly balanced distribution of tension, then tension in human musculature is the very opposite. Our fifth image is of a person disfigured by tension in their neck and permanently hunched shoulders, their held-in stomachs, their clenched jaws, their gripped fists (the list is not comprehensive). For Terry Schreiber tension comes with the territory since acting is 'one of the most stressful careers a person can choose'.[59] Laura Wayth notes that when an actor is tense they are cut off from their body, cut off from their impulses and thus are not 'physically free'. In such a state of paralysing tension the audience then focuses on the person of the actor on stage 'rigid, clenched, locked down, and "muscling up" his energy' rather than on their character.[60] Schreiber argues, 'Relaxation is the foundation for acting. All work stems from it. There is no possible way to reach the second step of acting – concentration – without being relaxed.' Echoing Wayth he contends that there 'is no way an actor can be open without minimising his body tension.'[61] All these writers argue that tension results in the actor not being able to transform their body (into that of a character): they are locked out of their imagination, closed, un-free.

So, what can an actor do about reducing or managing unwanted tension? Wayth argues, 'One of the goals of all physical acting training is to bring the actor to a kind of "physical neutral," a state where she can strip away all of her habitual tensions. Once the actor understands how to bring her own body to neutral, she can then layer other people's habits and physical characteristics on her blank canvas.'[62] Theresa Mitchell is one of the few theatre commentators who offer a physiologically detailed account of tension and relaxation: 'Muscles change their shape when flexing and contracting. A muscle never completely relaxes, and though you may be motionless, your muscles are always active. This is muscle tone, and it keeps your body in a continual state of readiness.'[63] While agreeing

---

[58]Grotowski 1979: 6.
[59]Schreiber 2005: 5.
[60]Wayth 2014: 182.
[61]Schreiber 2005: 3.
[62]Wayth 2014: 182.
[63]Mitchell 2009: 17.

completely about the importance of the aims of achieving physical neutrality (key to Jacques Lecoq's pedagogy) and readiness, the problem still remains *how* to achieve this balanced tensility? This book is not the place for discussion of practice, but it might come as no surprise that my main answer in *Training the Actor's Body* is the Feldenkrais Method and tai chi.

One final image of muscles. When I was in Beijing I met with a tai chi master who, when quizzed about muscles, stressed the importance of 'white muscle', a phrase that puzzled my translator. I realized that what he meant when I was watching David Attenborough explaining how it is that a frog can leap quite so far. He explains that when a frog sits, 'This stretches the leg tendons. Tendons are elastic like rubber bands. Stretching them stores energy within them. And then, when the frog jumps, the tendons release that energy, like firing a catapult.'[64] In terms of training I would think less about developing muscle bulk, and more about the tendinous tissue which joins muscles to bones and thereby enables movement.

Skin

> ... is the oldest and the most sensitive of our organs, our first medium of communication, and our most efficient protector [...] Even the transparent cornea of the eye is overlain by a layer of modified skin [...] Touch is the parent of our eyes, ears, nose, and mouth. It is the sense which became differentiated into the others, a fact that seem to be recognised in the age-old evaluation of touch as 'the mother of the senses.' (Ashley Montagu)[65]

Nowhere in my reading on actor training have I found a discussion of the skin: such an omission excludes the largest sensory organ in the human body. Thanks to receptors just beneath the skin we have our sense of touch which allows for the sensation of pressure guiding our knowledge of grip and contact in the fingers and hands, and balance in the feet (telling us where the weight falls on our soles); it helps us distinguish hot from cold, rough from smooth, wet from dry. Before organisms developed eyes or ears or nostrils they had cells in their skin that were sensitive to light, or to the vibrations of sound (deaf people can feel the vibrations of music through their skin), or to changes in the chemistry of the environment. Our outer layer is far from a crust beneath which lies our inner and sensitive self; it is the surface through which we sense changes in the world.

It is this surface sensitivity which prompted choreographer and teacher Dominique Dupuy to quote Paul Valéry's paradoxical *'Ce qu'il y a de plus profond*

---

[64]https://subsaga.com/bbc/documentaries/science/natural-world/2014-2015/10-attenboroughs-fabulous-frogs.srt
[65]In Pallasmaa 2009: 100–1.

en l'homme, c'est la peau. (The most profound thing about mankind is their skin.) We will see that this is more than a playful paradox and is a necessary corrective to Martha Graham who 'saw the skin solely as an envelope (movement understood as being within this envelope).'[66] Gerda Alexander emphasizes 'the astonishing significance of the skin as an organ, as a living envelope, with countless nerve-links throughout the whole organism. Contact through the skin, which gives us information about the outer world, makes us aware simultaneously of the essentials about ourselves. What we touch also touches us.'[67] Her words are in keeping with Dupuy who asserts, 'Man's skin is without doubt the most sensitive in the world; it isn't a carapace.'[68] Dupuy is right to provide a corrective to those who regard movement as coming from within, and ignore the contact and connection with the world of things and people within it.

Dupuy goes further by pointing out that there are two types of skin: the coarser skin of our back (*le peau dorsal*) and the more sensitive skin of our stomachs (*le peau ventral*). In Chinese this codes for *yang* (*dorsal*) and *yin* (ventral) and was also (according to my teacher Geraldine Stephenson) a distinction much used by Rudolf Laban. She would demonstrate raising the arms forward with the palms upwards (revealing the softer, *yin* skin), and the palms down (revealing the coarser, *yang* skin): the first suggested supplication, the second dismissal. We know this from daily life: the gesture of placing a hand on our back constitutes socially acceptable contact, but to touch the stomach is overly intimate. Something as basic as the sensitivity of different kinds of skin can promote different meanings in movement and social relations.

Deane Juhan argues, 'Touch, more than any other mode of observation, defines for us our sense of reality. As Bertrand Russell observed, "Not only our geometry and our physics, but our whole conception of what exists outside us, is based upon the sense of touch."'[69] A long paragraph in Merleau-Ponty's *Phenomenology of Perception*[70] discusses the relation of sight and touch. He begins with the infant's early explorations of the world through touch, which gradually expand into the world through finger-pointing at objects and people of interest, finally ending up as the direction of our eyes towards them. Merleau-Ponty explains how it is that our whole 'conception of what exists outside us' begins with the close-up scrutiny of touch and then extends to seeing which could be understood as kind of touching at a distance.

Juhan continues by observing how this physical connection with the things of the world also involves finding out about ourselves. To touch is not simply about

---

[66]Dupuy 2003 – Section on Skin.
[67]In Johnson 1995: 275.
[68]Dupuy 2003 – Section on Skin.
[69]In Johnson 1995: 275.
[70]Merleau-Ponty 1962: 222–5.

confirming the existence of these things, but also the nature of my own bodily existence.

> My sense of my own surface is very vague until I touch; at the moment of contact, two simultaneous streams of information begin to flow: information about an object, announced by my senses, and information about my body announced by the interaction with the object. Thus I learn that I am more cohesive than water, softer than iron, harder than cotton balls, warmer than ice, smoother than tree bark, coarser than fine silk, more moist than flour, and so on.[71]

Merleau-Ponty[72] explores this double sensation when he examines what happens when we press one finger against another: we are aware of one as the pusher (a motor sensation of exerting pressure) and the other as being pushed (a sensory experience).

These very fundamental discoveries are made at a very early age, and it is precisely these experiences that form the basis for the metaphors that Lakoff and Johnson describe as being our 'cognitive unconscious'.[73] They explain how 'We are physical beings, bounded and set off from the rest of the world by the surface of our skins, and we experience the rest of the world as outside us. Each of us is a container, with a bounding surface and an in-out orientation.' This orientation is then projected 'onto other physical objects' and as well as being imposed 'on our natural environment'.[74] Later they generalize about how we use bodily experience as a source of conceptual metaphor: 'since our brains are embodied, our metaphors will reflect our commonplace experiences in the world', with the most basic metaphors being 'universal because everybody has basically the same kind of bodies and brains and lives in basically the same kinds of environments'.[75] Without seeming to play with words, our sense-making should be understood as being both conceptual and sensory: here we are dealing with a very basic level of meaning and being.

Claxton goes further in explaining this sense of bodily connection with the world: 'We are "in touch" with the world by moving against it, and feeling it on our skin. Touch occurs when skin and world move relative to each other, and that gives us useful information.'[76] Later he discusses how the changes in the level of moisture in the skin can be tested by its electrical conductivity (electrodermal conductivity or EDA), which allows scientists to check on a person's reactions to events around

---

[71]Juhan in Johnson 1995: 369.
[72]Merleau-Ponty 1962: 94.
[73]Lakoff and Johnson 1980: 257, Lakoff and Johnson 1999: 5–12.
[74]Lakoff and Johnson 1980: 29.
[75]Lakoff and Johnson 1980: 257.
[76]Claxton 2015: 57.

them, reactions of which they may not be conscious, which is why he argues that 'EDA can be a more sensitive indicator of our thinking than our conscious minds are. Intelligence is a whole body happening.'[77]

One means of rethinking the actor's body is this expanded notion of intelligence. Sennett broadens the discussion by considering the skin as an 'ecological border' which he defines as 'a site of exchange where organisms become more interactive'. Our skin is that border at which world and self interact: 'An ecological border, like a cell membrane, resists indiscriminate mixture; it contains differences but is porous. The border is an active edge.'[78] These scientists, physical therapists and philosophers offer us a compelling reason to add the skin to our developing image of the actor's body. Although we may not realize it, this is a very basic means of connection with our fellow performers and the stage environment. We need to understand that our responsiveness (our responses) begin with our skin. In Chapter 4 I shall draw on some of the above information when we discuss training and sensitivity.

Summary

What does actor do with their body? They move. An examination of even the most basic organisms answers the question 'Why do we have a brain'? It is in order to move and to guide that movement. As organisms become more complex so they develop more complex forms of movement intelligence.

To explain the foundations of this movement intelligence some very simple organisms were studied –

- the sea squirt to demonstrate why need a brain;

- the sea snail to demonstrate how we learn;

- the tick to demonstrate the significance of a moment (the smallest amount of time of which we are conscious).

The basis of motor intelligence depends on the interrelation between motor and sensory nerves. Motor nerves cause muscles to contract and lengthen which when coordinated allow for purposeful movement. Sensory nerves provide information about the surrounding environment, and allow an organism to avoid threats and seek reproductive opportunities. Sensory and motor nerves communicate through synapses. Learning (i.e. memory) involves a strengthening in the synaptic connection (a change to the cell structure).

---

[77] Claxton 2015: 60.
[78] Sennett 2008: 227.

This local communication between nerves constitutes the broader connection between the organism and its environment. An organism is sensitive to what matters to it. This leads to the philosophical point that each organism is sensitive to its own world of objects. Things are perceived according to an organism's needs; perceptual capacities are adaptive. Uexküll defines a moment as that interval of time before something new is perceived as happening; for a tick this might last eighteen years, whereas for a human it is an eighteenth of a second.

Following from the questions posed in Chapter 1, Polyani's provocative statement that 'We know more than we can tell' was examined in further detail. The know-how of actors and craftspeople is called tacit knowledge. Explicit memory (or knowledge learned) takes verbal form and can be accessed consciously; tacit knowledge (of skills or techniques learned) can only be demonstrated through doing. To perform new skills fluently we have to become unaware of how they are performed: the body becomes absent which leads to the development of habits, which in turn requires regular training to remove those habits.

Three brief studies on feet, muscles and skin explore the above themes in the context of movement training for the actor.

- For Suzuki actor training begins with the feet.

- Bones are organs of compression – they take weight. Muscles are tensile, they move bones. The problem for the actor is unwanted tension.

- Skin, the most extensive sensory organ in the human is also the least recognised or understood. For Dominique Dupuy performer training should begin with the skin.

3 FRONT BRAIN/BACK BRAIN: THE EMBODIED BRAIN IN THEATRE AND NEUROSCIENCE

Introduction

The point of departure for this chapter's examination of bodily intelligence is the idea put forward in Clive Barker's *Theatre Games* that we have a front and back brain. By this means he offers an accessible if eccentric way of understanding how an actor can improve their speed of reaction (returning us to the theme of readiness) and become more aware of their surroundings. More generally, his distinction between front and back brain opens an overview into how the functions and structure of the mind and brain have been understood over the centuries. The chapter concludes with a consideration of the optimal state of consciousness or awareness the actor requires when performing.

I Front Brain and Back Brain

Theories of Mind: From Phrenology to Dynamic Systems

Most of us have seen white porcelain figures of the head divided into sections each marked with emotions, faculties and mental attributes. Although these heads are now bought as objects of curiosity, they were once considered as demonstrations of Franz Gall's science of phrenology. It might appear quaint to a twenty-first century reader that Gall should set out to find a correspondence between a person's behavioural and moral characteristics and the size of bumps on their head, but in other respects he was a serious anatomist and was the first physiologist to distinguish between grey and white matter in the brain. While there might be no correspondence between the outer contours of the skull and the brain beneath it, he was right to argue that the brain was the site of the higher mental functions like the mind.

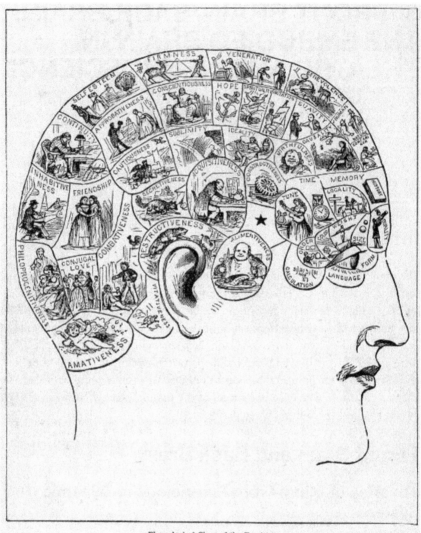

Phrenological Chart of the Faculties.

FIGURE 3.1 The Phrenological Head[1]

Gall's recognition of the importance of the brain contrasts with the practice of ancient Egyptians, who would preserve the dried organs of the kidneys, liver, intestines and stomach, each of which was placed in its own canopic jar, protected by its own deity while the heart, being the seat of thinking, was left in place. The brain, having neither function nor value, was unceremoniously drawn out through

---

[1]https://en.wikipedia.org/wiki/Phrenology.

the nose and discarded. If you have seen the wobbly white mass of a brain on television, then you might have some sympathy for the ancient Egyptian's attitude towards the brain. It is hard to believe that this strange pudding that lies bound in the darkness of a skull is responsible for our every action, thought and sensation.

Gall's theory was modular, proposing a one-to-one connection between a part of the brain and a function or emotion. It is an appealingly simple model taken from mechanics where one part has a specific role within the overall operation of a machine. Today we can see the same modular approach taken to genetics when newspaper headlines announce that the 'depression' gene (or even worse, the gay gene) has been 'identified'. In both cases the analysis is static and spatial rather dynamic and involving the dimension of time. The little I know about epigenetics is that it involves the time-based expression of a gene: that is, the gene may only become active when prompted by external circumstances; or, in terms of development, it may be turned off at a certain stage. For example, a gene responsible for the development of lungs is turned off at a certain moment in an axolotl which explains why it has external gills, whereas with newts the gene continues its function resulting in internal lung structures.

Once one introduces the dimension of time into descriptions of organic functions they are grasped as ongoing processes rather than once-only pictures. In Chapter 1 we saw Tononi and Edelman and Berthoz point to an ever more complex picture of neuronal activity. Humans have developed way beyond the simple neural structures of the sea snail or the tick: rather than thinking we have sensory and motor neurons located in parts of the brain dedicated to feeling and doing, we should now think that these functions are distributed throughout the brain, and that the relation involves rhythmic loops rather than straight lines. We need to think in terms of unpredictable dynamic systems rather than maps, and this means going beyond generalizations about front brain and back brain.

Clive Barker on the Front and the Back Brain

There are many references in *Theatre Games* to what Barker calls the front and back brain. His source for this knowledge of the brain was Moshe Feldenkrais's *Body and Mature Behaviour* (2005, first published in 1949). Barker had a gift for taking what he needed from quite complex theoretical texts and then explaining their ideas in an accessible way. He explains how the front part of his brain is used 'for visualising, for reflective meditation, for precisely defining my thoughts and ideas, for thinking in abstract, and for the deliberate conscious control and direction of my actions.' The back brain 'appears to control my physical actions and reactions instinctively without my being directly conscious of what is happening.'[2]

---

[2]Barker 2010: 17.

Throughout his book he returns to this basic division between a front brain which is engaged in conscious thinking and a back brain whose activities are undertaken non-consciously. For example, he will argue that 'if you let the back part of the brain work, without conscious interference, the body works more efficiently. If you concentrate on making the body work, you interfere with its working. […] Those who think, fail most often to gain the objective.'[3] The crucial point is to let the back brain work '*without conscious interference*'. One of his worst insults for a student was that (like me) they were intellectuals who were always 'overthinking' an exercise. In this he sees himself following Stanislavsky who was 'constantly trying to find ways for the actor to work through the subconscious mind/body mechanisms' rather than engaging 'the front brain.'[4] (I will discuss Stanislavsky later in this chapter.) The activity of the back brain is 'continuous, often tumultuous, and, largely, totally unconscious' and is revealed 'constantly and continuously' in our 'physical actions and purposes.'[5] In this portrayal of the back brain dealing with the body in action and the front brain dealing with the conscious mind, he evokes the familiar body-mind duality.

The brain is traditionally divided into three rather than two parts: the hind brain consists of the brain stem that rises from the spine, with the cerebellum attached to the rear; next is the midbrain; and then the mantle of the cortex (the forebrain) which lies on top.

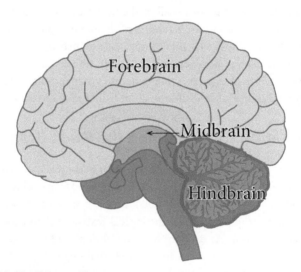

FIGURE 3.2 The Tripartite Brain.

---

[3]Barker 2010: 18.
[4]Barker 2010: 20–1.
[5]Barker 2010: 19.

This progression from hind brain to fore brain follows the evolution of the organ, with older parts of the brain dealing with automatic functions and the frontal cortex allowing for conscious control of many bodily functions. (As its title suggests, Elkonon Goldberg's *The Executive Brain* (2001) is devoted to explaining the role of the frontal cortex.) So, to some extent, Barker's analysis is right: the 'front' brain does correspond to conscious reflection and control (but not vision), while the functions of the 'back' brain remain inaccessible to consciousness. However, Barker is interested in what will help him better understand the work of the actor rather than in questions of neuroanatomy. One of the main questions he asks concerns the state of attention (another very important theme in *Training the Actor's Body*).

'Being in the Head' and 'Being in the Body'

To give an idea of how front and back brain operate Barker cites his experience of picking blackberries. He asks why it is that one so often misses a whole lot of berries that the next picker seems to notice and concludes that the 'technique is to watch the bush and the blackberries leap out at you'.[6,7] What prevents our seeing the berries is precisely the 'conscious interference' cited above: 'The act of consciously looking for something often restricts our response to the wide range of information that is present in any situation.'[8] Possibly he was here drawing on a principle that is central to Feldenkrais's theory of learning, that we cannot change anything through an act of conscious willing. As Feldenkrais trainer Carl Ginsburg explains, 'From his personal experience he knew that will power was not useful.' Rather, one had to exercise awareness, 'a consciousness with kinaesthetic knowledge, a listening to one's self while acting, a way of feeding back to one's self the state of one's system in functioning'.[9] Not surprisingly, Feldenkrais called one aspect of his method Awareness through Movement, also the title of one of his books (1980).

Barker seems to have grasped this distinction when he writes that a teacher needs 'to assist the actor to be aware rather than conscious of the way the mind and body co-ordinate naturally'.[10] In this elegant distinction between awareness and consciousness he is describing a soft as opposed to single focus,[11] a state of responsiveness, passive but not inert. In physical terms, this attentiveness is a state

---

[6]Barker 2010: 56.

[7]I used this quotation on page 47 of *Training the Actor's Body* when discussing Readiness and Soft Focus.

[8]Barker 2010: 56.

[9]Ginsburg 2005: xv.

[10]Barker 2010: 53.

[11]A theme that recurs throughout *Training the Actor's Body*.

of muscular tonus where one isn't held, stiff in conscious anticipation, but in a state of relaxed readiness (see the section on readiness in *Training the Actor's Body*).

Barker's distinction is valuable and it bears on the effective performance of movements. He argues that army instructors will tell recruits going round an obstacle course not to think about what they have to do, 'but just do it. Those who think, fail most often to gain the objective.'[12] Later, Barker concedes that conscious control 'when properly directed, often improves details here and there, but intellect is no substitute for vitality'. When he warns against 'over-taxing the conscious control with tasks the reflective nervous activity is better suited to perform'[13] he is drawing on his reading of Feldenkrais, although 'reflective nervous activity' doesn't seem a very accurate phrase.

Other teachers have written about this connection: Michel St Denis notes when an acting student focuses on 'technique' this disturbs 'the flow of his imaginative powers. It is only after the student has achieved a considerable mastery of all his expressive means that he will be able to accept technique and use it as an aid to his imagination.'[14] We will return to the question of learning in the head and learning in the body in the next chapter.

There is one further correlation to be explored: that between relaxation and soft focus. St Denis argues that the 'right kind of relaxation is a form of concentration; it is a condition of being *available,* of being ready to spring into action at any moment.[15] The 'condition of being available' means being ready both in time and space, and is a state of both mental and muscular ease. Writing of Viola Spolin, Laura Wayth observes, 'If an actor has to focus his attention fully on keeping a tennis ball in the air, there is no way that he can remain "in his head," focused on an intellectual concept or idea.' Spolin calls this 'direct experience' which she argues 'integrates mind and body, and produces spontaneous action and discovery in the act of doing'. Once again we see an opposition between doing and thinking, which characterizes Spolin's philosophy: rather than an intellectual approach she 'instead aims for experiencing something in the moment through play that opens up the actor's intuitive and holistic senses'.[16] Relaxation is at the nexus of several themes that will be discussed throughout this book: states of attention, states of tension, playfulness, ease and responsiveness, all of which are central to the training discussed in *Training the Actor's Body*.

John Lutterbie begins his book *Towards a General Theory of Acting* (2011) by comparing the working processes of two actresses, the first of whom works from scripts, the other taking a physical approach. What unites them is their

---

[12]Barker 2010: 18.
[13]Barker 2010: 31.
[14]St Denis 1982: 105.
[15]St Denis 1982: 106.
[16]Wayth 2104: 151.

rejection of the activities of the conscious mind: 'judging, self-judging, any mental activity, [...] any ego concerns, ideas of right and wrong choices' are referred to as 'clutter'. This analysis is very close to Barker's in its emphasis upon an avoidance of cognitive activity which thereby allows things to happen to you. The resulting attentive state is 'loose enough' to let the character in: 'There is an awareness that it happens, but that is what the "uncluttering" is: standing back and letting that happen.'[17] Whether it is a case of a character or blackberries, the approach is the same – let them come to you.

Lutterbie offers another way of grasping this opposition of 'being in the head' and 'being in the body'. Still writing about the two female actors he discusses the phenomenon of being in the moment, which he suspects 'is one of the more universal concepts in acting'. As far as these two actors are concerned, it is constituted 'by avoiding the intrusion of discursive thought, which is seen as a negative influence, as interfering with the actor's availability to unexpected images, as clutter that disrupts the reciprocal exchange between actors'. Barker doesn't use the phrase 'being in the moment' but in discussing this phenomenon we remain close to his conception of the desired attentional state of the working actor, particularly with the notion of discursive thought being an unwelcome intrusion. But it intrudes only in those moments of practical work in the studio: there is a place for reflection 'after the exercise is completed, whether in an improvisation or scene work'.[18]

Joseph Roach broadens this discussion of the attentional states of the actor by pointing out that soft focus is multi-modal. He describes the mental activity of an actor on stage as follows:

At any given moment the actor's mind must retain his cues, his lines, his blocking, his gestures, some idea of the similar assignments of his cohorts (lest they forget), audience reaction, the location of properties and their heft, the precise timing of complex business, and, if he works in that way, his motivation.[19]

The single focus of conscious attention is incapable of taking in all these activities with their respective spatio-temporal rhythms. An extreme example of this multi-focus was the feat of a performer called Ducrow who could ride six horses at once.[20] A more everyday example of this multi-attentional state can be found in Chapter 10 of Claxton's *Intelligence in the Flesh* (2015) which describes the amount of things that a waitress in a busy New York diner has to keep in her mind. Her description of how she walks recalls Barker's 'low centre': 'You learn

---

[17]Lutterbie 2011: 4.
[18]Lutterbie 2011: 4–5.
[19]Roach 1993: 190.
[20]There is a famous cartoon of this feat drawn by Robert Cruikshank in 1830.

a walk that gets you places quickly without looking like you are running .... This requires developing a walk that is all business from the waist down, but looks fairly relaxed from the waist up.'[21] The working centre is in the pelvis which allows the upper body to remain 'fairly relaxed'. Is there a research question here that might extend beyond the sphere of theatre and performance? This question concerns the correlation between body attitude and emotional/attentional state.

The Attentional State of Soft Focus: Neurological Accounts

The notion of unconscious readiness is not confined to theatre: in his book *Hare Brain, Tortoise Mind* (2000) Guy Claxton makes a plea for a slower, more responsive attitude towards the world where, as Barker put it, the 'blackberries leap out at you'. In a culture where time has become a commodity, there is no possibility of letting things come to you: one is constantly trying to force the pace, to make things happen. Claxton argues that 'modern Western culture' has lost its 'sense of the *unconscious intelligence* to which these more patient modes of mind give access' and 'has so neglected the intelligent unconscious – the *undermind,* I shall sometimes call it – that we no longer know we have it, do not remember what it is for, and so cannot find it when we need it.'[22] Although the undermind is not exactly the same thing as Barker's back brain, there is a broad similarity which I shall explore further.

In both Claxton's books (2000, 2015) he focuses on what he calls the 'inhibiting effect of intention', where, like Barker's blackberry-picker, we can't 'see for looking'. He wonders whether having to present an intention 'locks consciousness too firmly into a predetermined framework of plans and expectations, so that other information, which could potentially be useful or even necessary, is relegated to unconscious processes of perception, where it is, in these cases, ignored'.[23] Where Barker writes about conscious interference, Claxton writes about us using the deliberative mode where conscious intention leads our attention to *look for* rather than simply *look at* something. This conscious intention means that we will miss anything novel and only identify the predictable and already known. Such an approach is fundamentally uncreative.

Letting things come to you is a theme that runs through the arguments of many of the authors already cited. Claxton describes one of those visual puzzles where to start with you can only see marks on the page, but after a while the 'image' slowly lifts away from those seemingly meaningless marks. (This recalls the

---

[21]Claxton 2015: 222.
[22]Claxton 2000: 6–7.
[23]Claxton 2000: 129.

process described in Chapter 1 where we learn to distinguish the 'signal' of an object despite what Feldman Barrett calls the 'noisy information from our eyes, ears, nose and other organs'.[24]) He explains that the trick is not to look at the image 'with the normal high-focus gaze, scanning it for its "meaning,"' but if you 'relax your eyes so that they gaze softly *through* the image, and stay for while in this state of incomprehension, then the details begin to dissolve and melt into one another, and a new kind of seeing spontaneously emerges, one which reveals the "hidden depths" in the picture'.[25] This is an accurate description of the 'soft focus' I mentioned above. Edward Hall gives an example of his archaeology students not being able to 'see' arrowheads that were obvious to him when looking at the ground: 'Much to their chagrin, I would lean down to pick up what they had not seen simply because I had learned to "attend" to some things and to ignore others. I had been doing it longer and knew what to look for, yet I could not identify the cues that made the image of the arrowhead stand out so clearly'.[26] Hall offers another way of understanding the paradox of this kind of learning: although he was better at 'attending' to the search, he couldn't actually identify the cues by which he recognized the arrowheads. He knows how, but not what (to return to Ryle's elegant distinction).

In his most recent book, *Intelligence in the Flesh* (2015), Claxton further explores the 'skilled and variegated capability' which he calls attention, or 'learning by noticing'. Like Hall, he acknowledges that while he doesn't quite know how this faculty works, *it can be developed through practice*. Clearly it is a part of the deep structure of our brains: 'Just by being attentive to the world, the neurochemical systems pick up patterns and regularities. The body systems automatically tune themselves to register what goes with what, and what follows what.'[27] I shall return to this very important point below; in the meantime let us explore more examples of the faculty of attention.

Claxton cites the case of Karl von Frisch, the scientist who first noticed that bees returning to the hive perform a 'waggle dance' to tell their fellow workers where the pollen is. He commented, 'I discovered that miraculous worlds may reveal themselves to a patient observer where the casual passer-by sees nothing at all.'[28] Later Claxton comes close to echoing Barker when he notes that there are 'softer or "low-ego-control" versions of imagination in which we let things "come to us" in a state of relaxed but vigilant reverie.' And, yes, we can get 'better at slowing our thoughts and watching them unfurl from their embodied beginnings.'[29] This lends

---

[24]Feldmann Barrett 2017: 27.
[25]Claxton 2000: 174.
[26]Hall 1969: 69.
[27]Claxton 2015: 234.
[28]Claxton 2015: 235.
[29]Claxton 2015: 239.

support for the kind of training that, following Barker and Feldenkrais, I have being developing over the past twenty years. It rests on the belief (the hunch?) that in order to achieve certain skills, one has to learn how *not to try*. In *Training the Actor's Body* I cited Cicely Berry's advice on this point: "'Teach us to care and not to care,' as Eliot says. The "caring" is the work done to prepare, and the "not caring" is letting it go.'[30]

In the same vein, Juhani Pallasmaa writes admiringly about the designs of architect Alvar Aalto. Common to the examples given above, what characterizes Aalto's approach is the belief that 'in creative work a focused consciousness needs to be momentarily relaxed and replaced by an embodied and unconscious mode of mental scanning. The eye and the external world are dimmed for an instant, as consciousness and vision are internalised and embodied.'[31] Again, the emphasis is on embodiment and soft-focus, but Pallasmaa adds that 'in the midst of our labouring, calculating, utilitarian age, we must continue to believe in the crucial significance of play when building a society for human beings', concluding that 'we must combine serious laboratory work with the mentality of play, or vice versa.'[32] This is a theme that would surely appeal to the author of *Theatre Games*!

The notion of creative play brings us back to Claxton's notion of explorative messing about[33] whereby a person can make new discoveries about the world by a process of non-directed play conducted with awareness. This in turn links with Tim Ingold who discovered from the Saami people in Finland that it is 'by watching, listening and feeling – by paying attention to what the world has to tell us – that we learn'. Very much like Feldenkrais, who argued that we must learn how to learn, the Saami taught Ingold 'how I might find out'.[34] This multi-sensorial, playful attentiveness describes a bodily state in which creative affordances and discoveries can be made.

A common theme related to this sense of bodily attentiveness runs through the books of writers like Merleau-Ponty, Gallagher and Berthoz all of whom are trying to identify the meaning-making structures that lie beneath our consciousness. These are the neural structures that put like with like, that pick up patterns and regularities. Gallagher calls this a 'pre-theoretical' level of operation: the foundation on which conscious thought is built, indeed, the condition for conscious thought. In his *Phenomenology of Perception* Merleau-Ponty offers a variety of ways of grasping what he calls the '*preobjective view* which is what we call being-in-the-world'.[35] Claxton wrote about 'body systems' and Merleau-Ponty would argue that they exist in 'my organism, as a prepersonal cleaving to the general form of the

---

[30]Berry 1973: 19 (quoted on page 40 of *Training the Actor's Body*).
[31]Pallasmaa 2009: 74.
[32]Pallasmaa 2009: 76–7.
[33]Claxton 2015: 202.
[34]Ingold 2013: 1.
[35]Merleau-Ponty 1962: 79.

world' and thus play 'beneath my personal life, the part of an *inborn complex*'.[36] If this form of being in the world happens *before* our conscious life, it is also *beneath* it, being 'that primordial layer at which both things and ideas come into being'.[37]

While I realize this might be hard going for students of theatre, I do hope that I have conveyed the basic idea that we are dealing with a body system that pre-exists and makes possible our intellectual system. At the risk of trying the reader's patience I shall offer one last quotation from Merleau-Ponty because it sums up all the previous points:

> There is, therefore, another subject beneath me, for whom a world exists before I am here, and who marks out my place in it. This captive or natural spirit is my body, not that momentary body which is the instrument of my personal choices and which fastens upon that or this world, but the system of anonymous 'functions' which draw every particular focus into a general project.[38]

Here we have all the essential points about this pre-personal body, a body which is always there, always before those moments when I am aware of my body as an object, and thanks to whose structures and functions I *can* be aware of my body. This is an intelligence that is already at work before the ego has begun to work.

Front Brain/Back Brain: Neurological Accounts

While Barker's intuitions about the function of the mind may have been usefully informed by his reading of Feldenkrais, ultimately his 'neurology' has to be questioned. Barker has superimposed a seemingly scientific notion of brain structure upon the ancient oppositions between mind-body, human-animal and thought-feeling. In his modular approach Barker suggests that the actor has to suspend the activity of the front brain which 'gets in the way' of the more ancient, more animal and instinctual brain. It is as if these two parts of the brain work in isolation, one cancelling out the other. Norman Doidge argues that the three parts of the brain (forebrain, midbrain, hindbrain; see Figure 3.2) developed out of each other and that it is a fallacy to presume that 'when a new structure developed in evolution, it was simply added on to the older structure and that it now works independently of it'. This is a remnant of machine thinking where each working part has its discrete function. What really happened 'was that as a new structure was added, the older ones adapted; the presence of a new structure modified the old, and old and new *work together* holistically'.[39]

---

[36]Merleau-Ponty 1962: 84.
[37]Merleau-Ponty 1962: 219.
[38]Merleau-Ponty 1962: 254.
[39]Doidge 2015: 318–19.

Back we come to the recurring theme of holism: in theatre circles it is a pragmatic notion whereby the whole body is involved in an action; in neurophysiology it means that each part of the brain and the body works as an incredibly complex, self-regulating whole. Thus far from it being a question of either-or, Doidge argues, 'Our cortico-centric view has failed to take into sufficient account the contributions of the subcortical brain.'[40] Although theatre practitioners are the opposite of cortico-centric, they still undervalue the essential connection between parts of the brain. Edelman and Tononi's notion of 're-entry' has already given us an example of how functions are not localized, but can be parallel events in different brain parts some of which create looping connections with other parts and structures.[41]

Returning to the question of attention Doidge suggests that it is precisely one of these subcortical structures – the reticular activating system – which regulates our states of alertness and attentiveness. 'This activating system is nestled in the brain stem. It receives input from all the senses and processes the information to determine how awake or aroused and attentive a person should be.' He concludes

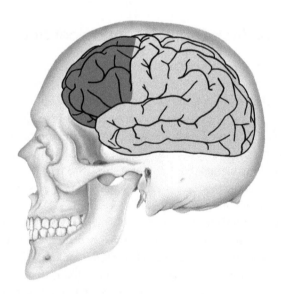

FIGURE 3.3 The Prefrontal Cortex.

[40]Doidge 2015: 318–19.
[41]Edelman and Tononi 2000: 49.

that it 'powers up the cortex from below'[42] – precisely the interaction between front and back which he was arguing for earlier.

There seems to be agreement amongst neurologists about how it is that we learn new kinds of movement. To put it in Clive Barker's terms, the information (be it visual or verbal) is first processed in the front brain, and gradually as the student masters the movement, so it is transferred to the back brain. Alain Berthoz explains that 'brain imaging has revealed that during motor training, the cerebral cortex is used at the beginning of the training and gradually becomes silent; the activity is then free to confront new problems and find new solutions to them'.[43] This model of learning is corroborated by neurologist Susan Greenfield who also notes while learning a task 'vast areas of the brain light up, particularly the prefrontal cortex'.

Once the skill 'has been practised enough to become second nature, many of these appear to shut down. The process becomes automatic, and the subconscious autopilot (which seems to involve the cerebellum) takes over.'[44]

Edelman and Tononi also note that the mastery of a skill consists of 'several repetitions under the continuous control of the conscious core'. The sign that a skill has been learned is when it can be performed 'error free'. They then describe how it is that just the required circuits that are selected and they alone are used; the rest, to use Greenfield's more accessible terminology, are 'shut down'. Here is how Edelman and Tononi put it:

> The portions of the brain responsible for the execution of each routine would soon be reduced to a specific and dedicated set of linked circuits. The resulting functional insulation would be ideal for optimising the neural interactions within such circuits while reducing those with the rest of the brain.[45]

This process is important to grasp since it underpins much of the argument about the learning of skills (or routines) in Chapter 4. The essential point to grasp is the reduction of brain areas 'responsible for the execution of each routine', and their functional insulation to maximize the neural interactions between these selected brain areas. While Greenfield suggests that these areas lie in the cerebellum, Edelman and Tononi suggest a structure called the basal ganglia – both being in what Barker would call the back brain.

---

[42]Doidge 2015: 339.
[43]Berthoz 2000: 237.
[44]Greenfield 2000: 172.
[45]Edelman and Tononi 2000: 188.

There Is No Little Person in Your Head

The image of the brain I have been trying to convey throughout this book is hard to grasp precisely because there is no obvious, linear connection between structure and function as there is in phrenology, or in Barker's notion of a front and a back brain. The problem is that we often think of understanding in terms of grasping something, holding it as a static image. With the brain we are dealing with an organ that works that engages in ever-changing – i.e. time-based – processes which are hard to visualize. Another way of approaching the difficult problem of understanding brain function as a dynamic process is to tackle two related problems: firstly, the (mistaken if widespread) notion that the brain operates by making mental representations of the outside world (something already challenged by Andy Clark), and secondly, that this notion presupposes a little person in the head who watches these images.

Claxton offers an accessible metaphor for understanding the operation of the brain. He begins by noting that the brain isn't 'organised into a neat series of processing steps, like an old-fashioned production line, that lead from perception, through thought and memory, to action'. This is the linear approach that Clark and Scott Kelso also criticize. Instead, Claxton suggests, 'Ears and Skin, Fingers and Shins, Lungs and Intestines' are all involved in 'a game of Chinese Whispers, with all chatting to each other'. He goes on that there is no separate compartment called memory, with memories and expectations being 'the stuff of all these conversations. And there is no Chief Executive who steps in to resolve disputes or correct impressions on the basis of her higher experience and intelligence.'[46] This is such a clear and accessible account of how the bodily organism operates without a little person in the head.

Since Lutterbie (2011) makes much use of Scott Kelso's *Dynamic Patterns* (1995), I shall consider some of his ideas about structure and function in the brain which develop Claxton's argument, although in a less accessible style. Scott Kelso argues against the notion of representation that is 'promoted by cognitive psychologists and artificial intelligence researchers'. A representation, he argues, 'is something that stands for something else; it is some kind of resemblance of the world outside stored inside the head'. He concludes that a 'representation is like a little person inside the head making sense of the meaningless sensations that impinge on the eye (or the ear, or the hand, or the nose)'.[47] Both he and Claxton reject our common-sense everyday notion of the world being represented in our brain for us (we are the little person). Once again we see a researcher questioning the notion that the world out there consists of finished images which we see

---

[46]Claxton 2015: 78.
[47]Scott Kelso 1995: 188.

through the windows of our eyes. I repeat Feldmann-Barrett's description of the 'noisy information from our eyes, ears, nose and other organs'[48] which it is the work of perception to render into recognizable sounds, smells and images. This is the pre-personal work that Merleau-Ponty described in Chapter 2.

Let us now explore how this argument against internal representations connects with Andy Clark's notion of the extended brain. His experiments with people playing Tetris on the computer revealed that the problem was not worked out *in their head* but on the screen, in the same way that Feynman's thinking took place on the page and not in his head. The *wirkraum* is out there in the world, and not in the head. This is a variation on the theme that subject and object, self and world, are not two separate things; to be a self is to be a body in a world. Had Barker known about this idea I feel sure he would have exclaimed – 'You see, this only proves my point that the actor must not be in their head!' His model of the brain does not lead to such a conclusion, but Clark's, Claxton's and Scott Kelso's do.

Having established that Scott Kelso is against representation, now to grasp what he is for. When he describes the brain (and its receptors and effectors) as 'fundamentally a pattern forming self-organised system governed by potentially discoverable, nonlinear dynamical laws a pattern-making organism' he introduces a lot of ideas that need explaining.

Humans Have Pattern-Forming Brains

We can all agree that humans see patterns in the outside world – it is a basic way of making sense out of the chaos of sense-data. In Chapter 2 Uexküll wrote about the mosaic (i.e. patterns) that we overlay on the outside world as 'a gift from the subject to things in its environment in visual as well as in tactile space, one which is not at all available in its surroundings'.[49] The constellations in the night sky are an example of us seeing (making up) patterns in the random scattering of stars.

When Scott Kelso touches on those potentially discoverable nonlinear dynamical laws, we start to get into quite difficult territory where 'behaviours such as perceiving, intending, acting, learning, and remembering' are described as being 'metastable spatiotemporal patterns of brain activity that are themselves produced by cooperative interactions among neural clusters'. Take a breath and read his description again slowly! Then, hopefully, you will see that it is only a more technical way of saying that behaviours are the result of patterns of activity across different parts of brain happening at different times. What we need to keep in mind is that 'Self-organisation is the key principle.'[50]

---

[48]Feldmann Barrett 2017: 27.
[49]Uexküll 2010: 60–1.
[50]Scott Kelso 1995: 257.

Scott Kelso also argues against the notion of the brain containing the operating programmes of a machine: 'It's not a static keyboard playing out a "motor programme" at all.'[51] This rethinking of our brain and body is far more complex than the common-sense image we have of them. Much of that complexity derives from (pre-personal) processes of which we are not conscious. One reason for this is that our reflective brain works far too slowly to pick up neural exchanges which last tens of milliseconds. To demonstrate this Scott Kelso notes that for a baby to make the sound 'ba' 'requires the precise coordination of approximately thirty-six muscles'. This might seem impossible, but then he explains that the production of a syllable like this 'requires the interaction among a large number of neuromuscular elements spatially distributed at respiratory, laryngeal, and oral levels, all of which operate on very different time scales. We breathe in and out roughly once every 4 seconds, the larynx vibrates at a fundamental frequency of about 100 times a second, and the fastest we can move our tongues voluntarily is about 10 repetitions a second'. And yet, despite all this complexity we still manage to articulate sounds that 'conform to a distinctive and well-formed pattern'.[52] We have to grasp that not only is the operation of our nervous system and our brain incredibly complex, but most of it is beneath our threshold of awareness. Of course, in our everyday lives we take our body and its functions for granted, but it is my contention that a better understanding of our bodily and neural structures might help us act more intelligently.

II Conscious or Unconscious?

Freud and Stanislavsky: Unconscious and Subconscious

Another mapping of the human mind is Freud's three-way division of ego, id and superego, which almost maps onto the medieval staging of the world, with the superego in the heavens, the ego as mankind on middle earth and the id as the devil who leaps about beneath the stage. Both operate on a metaphor where higher relates to the mental and the nonmaterial world, while lower means closer to the flesh and its urges, what Bakhtin (in a joyful reversal of this hierarchy) would call the 'lower material bodily stratum'.[53] Even if Freud and Barker use different axes, their divisions mark out similar territory: the front and top represents the conscious mind or ego, while the bottom and back represents the unconscious. Freud explains that the ego 'represents what may be called reason and common sense, in contrast to the id, which contains the passions'.[54]

---

[51]Scott Kelso 1995: 262.
[52]Scott Kelso 1995: 40.
[53]See in particular Chapter 6 of *Rabelais and His World*: Images of the Material Bodily Lower Stratum.
[54]Freud 1961: 25.

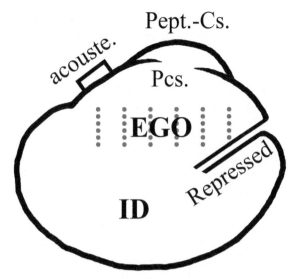

FIGURE 3.4 Freud's Image of the Superego, Ego and Id[55]

To describe how the ego keeps the id in check Freud uses the image of a rider trying to keep a horse on a tight rein. Those familiar with Plato might detect an echo of his *Phaedrus* where the soul (ego) is a charioteer who has to rein in two very different horses: one representing reason (superego) which is easily controlled, the other representing the irrational passions (id) which is harder to control. However, Freud argues that if a rider doesn't want to be thrown from their horse, they are 'obliged to guide it where it wants to go; so in the same way the ego is in the habit of transforming the id's will into action as if it were its own'.[56] Where Plato demands mastery over the irrational passions, Freud argues for a more accommodating coexistence between reason and instinct. The important point to be made is that this top/bottom, front/back division is between an executive centre for reason and another part of the brain which is more instinctual. Like Freud, Stanislavsky made use of the same mapping of the brain: two levels separated by an invisible threshold.

Stanislavsky uses the term 'subconscious' for that part of the mind dealing with instinct, inspiration and intuition with the prefix 'sub-' suggesting that this faculty, like Freud's id, lies beneath the threshold of conscious thinking. Although the contents of 'subconscious' and 'unconscious' differ considerably, the interest of both Freud and Stanislavsky lies in this lower level of consciousness. However, Stanislavsky's interest in the subconscious, indeed in the mind, fell foul of official

---

[55]By Sigmund Freud – http://www.freud.org.uk/about2.html[dead link], Public Domain, https://commons.wikimedia.org/w/index.php?curid=9966760.
[56]Freud 1961: 25.

Soviet psychology which, as Benedetti explains,[57] was strictly behaviourist (as mentioned earlier, Pavlov's approach became the official Soviet psychology in 1934).

In his final drafting of *An Actor's Work*, Stanislavsky was obliged to rewrite sections devoted to the subconscious, especially Chapter 16, titled as it was 'The Subconscious and the Actor's Creative State'. Smeliansky cites an admission that references to the spirit and soul were bound to get him into trouble with the Soviet censors: 'To my mind, the greatest danger of the book is "the creation of the life of the human spirit" (you are not allowed to speak about the spirit). Another danger: the subconscious, transmission and reception, the word *soul*. Wouldn't that be reason to ban the book?'[58] No wonder that these thoughts which were written during Stalin's Great Purge of 1936–8 remained unpublished: any reference to the 'living human spirit' or the 'human soul' would have been suicidal.

In unpublished notes for his Introduction to *The Actor's Work* Stanislavsky expresses alarm at the 'kind of scientific sophistries actors use at moments when they are creating intuitively, and it is that with which this book is mainly concerned.' This is a critical point for him – and one probably directed at his student Vsevelod Meyerhold who proposed a more scientific, biomechanical approach – since 'Acting is above all intuitive, because it is based on subconscious feelings, on an actor's instincts.' Although elsewhere he shows a degree of respect in and curiosity about the workings of the brain, ultimately Stanislavsky argues, 'Intuition must be the bedrock of our work, because our constant concern is the living human spirit, the life of the human soul.' The actor's work is created through feeling and can be summed up in three words: 'knowing means feeling'.[59] As we explore Stanislavsky's ideas about the mind and creativity we will see that he is not interested in creating anything like a systematic theory of mind; terms and ideas are deployed in a pragmatic search for how he can better understand the actor's work.

Stanislavsky almost goes so far as to express an interest in neurophysiology when he wonders where intuition, inspiration, the subconscious 'are lodged in us'.[60] He offers three alternatives: first, they are outside the mind being the gift of the Muses; second, they exist in the heart (an opinion one can still hear voiced); thirdly, they are located in the brain. In elucidating the relation between the conscious and subconscious mind he turns to another metaphor: consciousness is 'a light thrown on a particular spot in our brains, illuminating the thought on which our attention is concentrated'. Pragmatic to the last, he then asks, 'But does

---

[57]Benedetti 2008: xvii.
[58]Smeliansky 2008b: 689.
[59]Stanislavsky 2008b: xxiv.
[60]Stanislavsky 2008b: 296.

that advance the practical side of the matter for us? Has anyone learned how to control this flashing light of our subconscious, our inspiration or intuition?'[61]

If there are similarities between Freud and Stanislavsky, they are outweighed by the differences. Freud began work as a neurophysiologist before developing a theory of mind which centred upon an unconscious whose contents are irrational and sexual and therefore have to be repressed; they are unrepresentable. Stanislavsky's vision of the subconscious was less to do with sexual repression than creativity, 'That is why I maintain that in life the subconscious and we are good friends.'[62] Although both might agree that the subconscious is the zone of the instinctual, they have different visions of instinct. For Stanislavsky (and to an extent Grotowski after him) the inner life of the subconscious brought one in contact with (true) nature, with the freed creative spirit. The function of the conscious mind is not to repress the sexual instincts of the id but to offer 'pathways to the threshold of the subconscious which alone form the real basis of theatre'.[63] Elsewhere, he explains that creative work proceeds only 'partially under the direct guidance and influence of the conscious mind. It is, for the most part, subconscious and involuntary.' He then reveals the true source of creativity: 'the most miraculous of artists – nature. Not even the most refined technique can be compared to her. She holds the key!'[64] The ego (the conscious, deliberating self) is something that gets in the way of the source of creativity: 'nothing prevents nature from working freely, at her own discretion, in accordance with her needs and desires.'[65] Can we not see in Stanislavsky's rather romantic vocabulary an echo of Claxton and Barker who advise that we let the blackberries come to us, rather than consciously seeking them out. Is there a connection between Stanislavsky's subconscious and Claxton's 'undermind'?

This 'naturalness' of attitude is at the heart of Stanislavsky's approach to acting when he advises that actions performed 'directly, sincerely' would bring 'nature and the subconscious into play quite normally', and in this way students would be able 'to release the excess tension which was preventing genuine, productive, specific action'.[66] While Stanislavsky would argue against there being any *direct* way to the creative subconscious, his notion of the 'psychotechnique' offers an *indirect* one. The basic task of this psychotechnique 'is to bring the actor to the state in which his creative subconscious can burgeon', later noting how it stimulates the actor's 'natural, subconscious creative powers'.[67] The emphasis

---

[61]Stanislavsky 2008b: 296.
[62]Stanislavsky 2008b: 328.
[63]Stanislavsky 2008b: 346.
[64]Stanislavsky 2008b: 17.
[65]Stanislavsky 2008b: 335.
[66]Stanislavsky 2008b: 599.
[67]Stanislavsky 2008b: 329.

throughout his argument is about allowing a natural process to happen; it is about creating 'the favourable conditions in which the work of nature and the subconscious can take place'.[68] (This connects with how both Feldenkrais and Barker taught: in their lessons and games they would create the conditions in which a student could learn.) Towards the end of *The Actor's Work* he explains how this technique addresses the single greatest challenge to the live performer: they have to be creative at a certain time and place. Thus things 'which happen spontaneously in life, onstage often need the help of our psychotechnique which teaches us to perform all the moments, phases in our organic processes, including *communicating,* consciously'.[69]

As I noted in *Training the Actor's Body* much training focuses less on adding than in taking away, in learning how to avoid getting in your own way.[70] I explained in my earlier book that not just Grotowski's *via negativa* but Timothy Galwey's 'inner game' and much of Feldenkrais's Method are based on removing impediments to your natural ability to do things. We will return to this idea of allowing things to happen (naturally) in both Chapters 5 and 6 where the notion will be expressed in terms of trying to avoid blocks in the circulation of our (creative or vital) energy. In Chapter 8 we revisit the theme when we deal with stage fright; precisely that 'excess tension which was preventing genuine, productive, specific action' described above by Stanislavsky.

Not Knowing How We Do What We Do

In a chapter about front and back brain we should remember that much of the activity of the brain is not accessible to conscious reflection. Were it so we should simply be too late! And even when we are conscious of our actions, often they are best performed unguided by the conscious mind. Philosophers Gilbert Ryle and Shaun Gallagher both choose to illustrate this point by discussing our ability to drive without thinking about it. Ryle explains how a careful driver does not actually imagine or plan for all 'the countless contingencies that might crop up', but if a runaway donkey strays onto the road they are not 'unprepared for it' and possess a 'readiness to cope with such emergencies'. And yet all the while the driver chats to their passenger 'when nothing critical is taking place'.[71] Gallagher notes that we can drive perfectly safely and yet we may not remember the journey. This does not mean that 'the driver has been unconscious or has paid no conscious attention to driving', but rather that it is 'much more efficient and less dangerous

---

[68]Stanislavsky 2008b: 337.
[69]Stanislavsky 2008b: 624.
[70]McCaw 2016: 152.
[71]Ryle 1966: 47.

that we quickly forget what we have just done and focus on what is present and just about to occur'.[72]

Several important points are being made here. Firstly, that a careful driver is better prepared for the unexpected by not planning and imagining all unforeseen contingencies *in their head*. To return to Andy Clark's idea of the extended brain, a driver's mind needs to be on the road which is where the information is. And they need a soft focus to be able to respond with speed (rather than consciously running through scenarios in their head). Gallagher also argues it is safer that our mind is uncluttered with details of where we have been so we can focus on what is in front of us. They make a similar point to Barker's story of picking blackberries – we need to let non-conscious processes do their work.

Drew Leder observes that even a simple an activity like walking cannot be undertaken consciously because it is just too complex. Even if I could consciously manipulate 'all the proper muscles, I would soon find myself incapacitated', but 'if I tried to initiate my stroll by explicitly sending out certain nerve signals from the cerebral cortex, I would not even know how to begin. All our scientific knowledge does little to change this situation.'[73] Leder describes a similar level of same complexity to that of the baby making the sound 'ba'. This is an important caveat about the limit and applicability of science in the field of performance and theatre. The body has to be 'absent' to the moving person because of the inherent complexity of its operation.

Leder concludes, 'Our lived mentality cannot simply be equated with brain function but is ultimately distributed throughout the body.' This notion of the 'distributed brain' echoes Frank Wilson's expanded notion of the brain which 'reaches out to the body, and with the body it reaches out to the world'[74] and with earlier definitions of the body as being shaped by the environment. Leder continues:

It is not the brain alone that formulates speech, turns a discerning eye upon the environment, moves intelligently to accomplish its projects. For this, mouth, eye, and limbs are needed as well, our entire corporeal presence taking in and acting upon the world. The lived body is mentalised through and through, all of its organs participating in a uniquely human intelligence.[75]

What a great phrase: 'the lived body is mentalised through and through'. It is this process of 'mentalization' that renders the body alive, present, to the moving subject and that allows that moving subject to know him- or herself as a whole,

---

[72]Gallagher 2005: 58, note 163.
[73]Leder 1990: 20.
[74]In Ingold 2013: 112.
[75]Leder 1990: 114.

or as Leder puts it, an 'entire corporeal presence'. This adds an important new dimension to the discussion of wholeness. Here the idea is not mechanical and not figurative, but rather the body is experienced as a whole thanks to the integrative activity of the brain extended throughout the body via its nerves. A final aspect of this wholeness is that body and mind are seen to operate together – they cannot do otherwise. A body without nerves and brain is inert and dead to itself. This is a corrective to a notion that is popular within the physical theatre community that only once the conscious mind is silenced can the body truly speak. It is for this reason that I suggest that we start to talk about the body and the brain rather than the body and mind (or bodymind, or any such variation). This line of thinking might lead to a greater understanding of the actor's work, and how this work can be understood in a wider context. In Mark Evans's *Movement Training for Modern Actors* he asks whether the body has 'its own form of intelligence?'[76] Not only does Leder answer in the affirmative, but he also accounts for the source of this intelligence, what he calls 'the mentalised body'.

Summary

Front and Back Brain – Against a Modular Brain – An Orchestral Conception of Body and Brain

Barker's division of the brain into two parts – front and back – prompted a wider discussion of the merits of such mapping of brain function. Based on the foregoing argument I would now argue that there are no 'equals' signs in nature; we must resist the temptation to create reductive maps where we declare that this part of the brain *equals* that function. If we have learned anything from this chapter, it is that the nervous systems of higher animals are mind-bogglingly complex. To understand the vital processes of living creatures we need to include the dimension of time. As movement expert Warren Lamb[77] loved to say, 'Movement is a process of variation.' In his beautiful little book *The Music of Life* (2008) cardiologist Denis Noble argues that maybe we should think of vital processes as a complex musical texture unfolding over time.

Notions of Time – The Now of Presence – Flow

Another aspect of time was the notion of being in the moment: an experience that is central to the mentality of the performer (certainly in the performing arts, but maybe also in sports?). This brings together a number of important themes. To

---

[76]Evans 2009: 83, 89.
[77]See the section 'Movement Is a Process of Variation', in *Training the Actor's Body* (2018), p. 173ff.

be present in the moment is to be aware, alert, available, and to possess a certain sense of presence. Csikzentmihalyi's classic study *Flow* (2009) goes some way to explaining this state of being present in the moment, what he would describe as moment of flow (it is a 'sweet spot' that lies between anxiety and boredom: too easy a task and we are bored, too hard and we become anxious).

States of Attention – Receptive Passivity – The Undermind – Embodied Meaning

Related to this sense of presence is the state of attentiveness. I used Barker's example of picking blackberries to illustrate a state of receptive and non-directed attention. Where Barker attributes this state of patient and receptive noticing to the back brain (in Chapter 6 we will see him relate this to the lower bodily centre), Claxton relates it to the undermind. Terms like *sub*conscious and *under*mind operate on the topographic notion that our mind is organized vertically, with the higher mental functions being intellectual and cognitive, the lower being bodily and instinctual. Barker and Claxton would suggest that the interesting work happens not at the level of intellectual (and unembodied) thinking but rather at a lower, more embodied level. It is at this level of operation that I think we can discover a bodily intelligence. Indeed (as Barker, Claxton and others have argued), thinking can get in the way of this intelligence, of this state of spatial and temporal presentness, of being aware of and through the body. I would go further in this analysis and argue that we are talking about a kind of bodily creativity that is involved in discovery and problem-solving.

Complexity – Even the Simplest of Tasks Is Bewilderingly Complex

Even if Barker's neurology is fanciful and inaccurate, neurophysiologists agree that much of our motor activity is conducted beneath our level of conscious awareness (in the lower brain structures and the cerebellum – i.e. the 'back brain'). Scott Kelso, Leder and Sweigard demonstrated how the complexity of human movements means it cannot be conducted consciously. Remember it takes thirty-six muscles to pronounce the sound 'ba'!

4 'BODY/THINK': BEING, SENSING, KNOWING

Introduction

How do we know our own bodies, how do we know through our bodies and in what does this knowledge consist? This chapter divides into three parts: the first being concerned with *how* we know what it is to be an embodied being, the second addressing *what* kind of knowledge this involves and the final part discussing how we embody this knowledge. Ultimately, because we are dealing with a different kind of knowing (non-propositional, non-symbolic, non-linguistic) we find ourselves describing and defending a very different kind of knowledge, of learning and way of recovering that knowledge.

I Being in Your Body

What is it to be 'in your body'? Are there degrees to which an actor is in their body? In *Training the Actor's Body*[1] I quoted a comment made by Peter Brook to actors during an exercise. He asked them to make a gesture without asking '"What does it mean?" in an intellectual and analytical manner, otherwise you will remain on the "outside."'[2] Brook is suggesting that to be in your head (consciously trying to work out meanings) necessarily means that you are not in your body. Although this might seem to suggest a kind of mind/body dualism (which in turn underpins the inside/outside split), I am more interested in how it opens the question about what it is to 'inhabit' one's body – an expression used by both neuroscientists and theatre practitioners.

There are several dimensions to the problem of inhabiting our body. Firstly, we can transcend our immediate surroundings by acts of thought or imagination; we can 'forget' ourselves when we enter a thinking state and become oblivious to our surroundings. The problem could be expressed in terms of states of attention:

---

[1]McCaw 2018: 62.
[2]Brook 1993: 69.

either the actor approaches the question of the meaning of gesture mentally (imagining what they look like doing it, or how it might be interpreted by another) or they simply examine what it feels like when it is being performed. The questions in this chapter address a certain kind of attention, of presence, which is to do with a connection, a moment of conscious experiencing of the body. How does this tally with what an actor knows? They 'know' how other people move and act. Theirs is a bodily knowing; and, as Polyani says, they know more than they can tell.

Floyd Ruhmor argues that we are in our bodies when 'every aspect of your inner world coexists with every aspect of your outer world. The body is constantly acquiring knowledge.'[3] This tallies with Brook's analysis: he notes the 'true actor recognises that real freedom occurs at the moment when what comes from the outside and what is brought from within make a perfect blending'.[4] Another aspect of this experience is that our awareness of all parts of our bodies – including 'back of legs, inner thighs, and the oblique muscles that are often neglected'[5] – is awakened. Litz Pisk, a legendary teacher of movement, adds that you 'inhabit your body by your presence in it and by your awareness of it'. She develops the all-important question of inner and outer when she notes: 'You do not watch it from the outside, arrange yourself in front of the mirror, stand or walk next to yourself, observe and analyse, but connect yourself with your body and feel for an inner rightness.'[6] 'Inner rightness' is a very useful phrase to remember. Pisk also points out that when 'divorced from the body' the brain becomes 'the great dictator, doubter and dissector who cuts your body and its movements to pieces'.[7]

Brook, Pisk and Ruhmor pose a number of important questions about how an actor can know their own body. They all agree on two principles: that an actor needs to learn how to 'inhabit' their body (as opposed to seeing it from the outside in a mirror, or by imagining it) and that this is not an easy state to achieve: it requires work. Ruhmor describes inhabiting as a state where the whole body is awakened, Pisk as a state of presence and awareness. Both develop the theme that to know the body is to achieve this state of inner occupation or awareness. Quite *how* the actor learns to develop this awareness (a central element of the Feldenkrais Method, one half of which consists of lessons in Awareness through Movement™) is discussed fully in Chapters 5 and 6 of *Training the Actor's Body*.

Lorna Marshall's *The Body Speaks* offers a parallel concept to Barker's body/ think, where, the duality of body and conscious mind is presented more explicitly as a conflict. She describes how an actor's conscious brain can believe 'that everything is under control' at the same time that 'your body is telling you

---

[3]In Potter 2012: 22–3.
[4]Brook 1993: 69.
[5]In Potter 2012: 22–3.
[6]Pisk 1998: 11.
[7]Pisk 1998: 9.

that things aren't that simple'. This conflict, she continues, is an example of 'the non-verbal intelligence processing information. Intelligently and efficiently, but bypassing language. And the body is able to access this area of knowledge and experience.'[8] The writers quoted so far may be using theatrical terms that do not stand up to scientific scrutiny, but as I shall argue presently, the difference between their image of brain function and that of the scientists lies more in the use of metaphor and terminology than actual neurological fact. Thus when Marshall writes about 'non-verbal intelligence' or Barker about body-think, we will find that writers like Claxton, Ingold and Sennett support such concepts. Their support comes in great part because these more scientifically oriented commentators have all declared an interest in what one might call 'practitioner wisdom'; just look at their titles, *Intelligence in the Flesh, Making, The Craftsman*.

The practitioner vocabulary used thus far can be found in much of the literature that I surveyed for *Training the Actor's Body*. But while we have touched on an intelligence that comes through actively being in the body, we have only begun to tease out some of the knots in this complex problem. Marshall's mention of accessing an 'area of knowledge and experience' links back to Ruhmor's notion that the 'body is constantly acquiring knowledge'. These statements prompt a series of questions about this way of knowing (through feeling and sensation) and what knowledge is being revealed thereby.

Ruth Foster (vice principal of Dartington College of Arts in the 1960s when it began to champion somatic studies) wrote a book called *Knowing in My Bones* (1976) where she states that performers do not know 'analytically, but in their bones'.[9] Her book is a compendium of practitioner knowledge, garnered through extensive interviews. She cites Jane Howell, a director for stage and television who remembers her experience of studying drama at university: 'I understood it in my head [...] but it's taken me ten years to understand it in my body. It's not until you meet that situation yourself that you find you can understand anything.'[10] Later in her book Foster further explains this type of knowing: 'That which we know in our bodies is knowing that has been absorbed into the fabric of our being. It underlines our attitudes, our awareness of ourselves, and of the world that we inhabit.'[11]

Drew Leder explains that this kind of embodied knowledge marks the shift from 'I can' (where one is conscious of one's skill or knowledge) to 'I do' (where it has become a way of being who you are and how you live). The skills that we have learned over time 'simply disappear from view. They are enveloped within the structure of the taken-for-granted body from which I in*habit* the world.'[12] This

---

[8]Marshall 2001: 85.
[9]Foster 1976: 82.
[10]In Foster 1976: 66.
[11]Foster 1976: 112.
[12]Leder 1990: 32.

is more than agile wordplay. He is describing the process by which knowledge becomes 'tacit', which again returns us to Polyani's famous dictum – We know more than we can tell. Put another way, once knowledge has become embodied – has become 'muscle memory' – it thereby becomes inaccessible to the conscious mind. Thus we are returned to the idea that 'the body' knows but cannot tell, and when mind is involved it just seems to get in the way of the body's way of knowing. Although I do not entirely subscribe to this idea, I shall leave the matter here for the moment.

Becoming 'Quite Simply More Sensitive'

When one does exercises, it isn't to make people more powerfully skillful, it's to make everybody from the start quite simply more sensitive.[13]

I quoted Peter Brook's words in *Training the Actor's Body* where I argued that most chapters in that book 'could be understood as developing a sensitivity to some particular aspect of the actor's work on their body – to ensemble, to the structure of one's joints, to one's sense of gravity, to how one breathes and sounds that breath, to different qualities of movement, to space and finally to rhythm and pacing.' Following Brook, I regard one of the main ends of training as developing our faculty for sensing different aspects of our movement and our modes of action. Through developing an ever finer awareness or sensitivity to how one uses oneself, one can continue to learn and develop as an artist. Sensitivity is not a given faculty, but one that can and must be developed. Behind Brook's conception of training lies a rather different notion of the body: it is not a machine for movement or work consisting of muscles to be built, bones to be strengthened, and tendons and ligaments to be warmed up, but rather a sensing device that is aware of the affect and effect of its every movement. Underlying this conception is the idea of the body being the actor's instrument; but an instrument of what? Is it (returning to the argument of Chapter 2) purely a mechanical effector, or is it a gauge of the effectiveness of those movements, or again, a detector of the affect generated by those movements? By extension we can then ask whether the movement training of an actor is about being able to perform movements (higher, quicker, lower, etc.) or to become more sensitive to how those movements are performed?

In a similar spirit, Elsa Gindler (1885–1961), a pioneer of body-work, declares that her *Gymnastik* 'is not the learning of certain movements, but rather the achievement of concentration.'[14] Again, the emphasis is not on motor output but on a mental state that informs and is informed by movement. She expands upon

---

[13]Brook 1994: 7.
[14]In Johnson 1995: 5.

this very subtle distinction: 'We see to it that our students do not learn an exercise; rather, the *Gymnastik* are a means by which we attempt to increase intelligence.' She explains that her exercises in breathing are a 'means of our getting acquainted with the workings of our lungs, either through inducing or releasing holdings'.[15] Put another way, her exercises help us become more aware, more sensitive to how we breathe, an activity to which we usually pay no attention. The exercises or tasks she sets have to be 'executed thoughtfully, and when we are contented with ourselves in the doing, we experience consciousness'.[16] Gindler describes a state of attentiveness, of awareness that is very close to the passive receptiveness described by Barker when picking blackberries. The aim of training is to achieve a state of consciousness that is less goal-driven, a permissive state of awareness where the nature of one's physical activity can become clearer to oneself. In this way one can develop the somatic (i.e. bodily) intelligence that Mark Evans was writing about in his book on movement training for actors (2009).

Jacques Lecoq (whose school had a close relationship with Brook's theatre *Bouffes du Nord* in Paris) broadens the field of sensitivity even wider. One aim of his training is to help the actor learn 'to sense all the fine shades of difference which separate one material from another or which co-exist within the same material. Substances which are doughy, unctuous, creamy, oily, all possess different dynamics.' Typically Gallic, he declares his aim 'is for the students to acquire a taste for such qualities, exactly as a gourmet will recognise the subtle differences between flavours. To do so involves hard work over a long period, going on to colours, lights, words, rhythms, spaces.'[17] As in any training, his aim is to broaden the student's capacity; in this case it is to develop a finer, more discriminating sensorium, which, as he points out, 'involves hard work over a long period'. His insistence upon 'work' should remind us of the effort of sensing, an ability that has to be developed and informed. It is this work that transforms the chaos of sensory data into information.

Roland Barthes captured this different feel for learning in his inaugural lecture to the College de France when he declared that he was more interested in *saveur* than *savoir*, savouring words rather than being 'savvy' about them.[18] The accent once again is on the engagement of the senses.

Rhonda Blair and Sharon Carnicke both make some fascinating points about how feeling and consciousness are conceived in the Russian language. The Russian noun for consciousness 'is *samochuvstvo* – literally "self (*sam*)-feeling (*chuvtsvo*)," i.e. the feeling, or experiencing, of a self'.[19] The Russian verb *chuvstvovat'* 'is

---

[15]In Johnson 1995: 7.
[16]In Johnson 1995: 6.
[17]Lecoq 2000: 44.
[18]Barthes 1978: 21.
[19]Blair 2008: 58.

remarkably extensive in its possible meanings: "to feel," "to have sensation," "to be aware of," "to understand."[20] The meanings of this verb very precisely encompass what I have been trying to describe and could be summed up as the capacity to make sense of our bodies moving in the world.

Stanislavsky uses the term 'psychophysical' to express this connection between the mental (understanding) and the physical (sensing): 'In every physical action there is something psychological, and in the psychological something physical.'[21] Carnicke explains how Stanislavsky uses the verb 'Vchuvstvovanie' – literally, 'to feel into' – to describe how an actor can get into the feeling state of a character. But how does an actor truthfully embody a character over successive performances? In an unpublished manuscript Stansilavsky explains that 'it is necessary to experience the role, that is, to have the sensation (obschushchat') of its feelings, every time and on every repetition of creativity'.[22] In other words, the actor's body has to develop a sensitivity in order to be able to feel into a character. We now turn to the more specialized sensitivity to movement.

The Kinaesthetic Sense and Body/Think

Clive Barker's concept of body/think[23] covers quite a range of perceptual activity. He begins by suggesting this is another, more accessible, term for the kinaesthetic sense which he defines as 'the process by which we subconsciously direct and adjust the movements of our bodies in space, either in response to external stimuli, or to intentions arising in the mind' and then lists others:

> … the process by which physical purposes are carried out effectively for the greater part of our lives;
> … the process by which we practise habitual physical skills naturally and unselfconsciously;
> … the process by which we constantly take in information from the external environment and react to it without reflection, and by which we comprehend and respond to information being sent to the brain by our own bodies.[24]

None of these four processes quite tally with the *Oxford English Dictionary*'s definition of the kinaesthetic sense: 'The sense of muscular effort that accompanies a voluntary motion of the body. Also, the sense or faculty by which such sensations are perceived.' While the *OED* definitions focus on the sense of

---

[20]Carnicke 1998: 139.
[21]Carnicke 1998: 139.
[22]Carnicke 1998: 49.
[23]Barker 2010: 29, 64, 128, 137, 138, 160.
[24]Barker 2010: 29.

movement, Barker is concerned with the conduct, direction and adjustment of actions; later he writes about 'non-reflective body/think mechanisms'[25] and the 'body/think reflex ability',[26] both of which concern the execution rather than the sense of movement. Far from being about the kinaesthetic sense, his notion of body/think is much closer to the activity of what he calls the 'back' brain. It is too easy to pick holes in Barker's very home-made approach to understanding the operation of the actor's body (and brain) in action. But he was on the right path in trying to identify a kind of embodied thinking, one that made sense of the work of the actor, and just as importantly, makes sense for the actor.

If there are few references in the literature on actor training to the kinaesthetic sense as such, there is broad agreement that the actor needs to be aware of how they move. C.J. Gill argues that unless you 'are sensitive to your feeling for your own movement, [how] can you perceive accurately the significance of the movement of others?'[27] Barker would surely agree: he and Brian Murphy would spend hours people-watching.[28] Mary Fliescher observes that 'our connection to the performer is a kinaesthetic one, as we watch a body not unlike our own breathing and held in space, still in a dynamic relationship to gravity'.[29] Both people-watching and spectating rely on the activity of mirror neurons. As already noted, McConachie and Hart argue that the empathetic observation of 'most spectators' is 'a mode of cognitive engagement involving mirror neurons in the mind/brain that allow spectators to replicate the emotions of a performer's physical state without experiencing that physical state directly'.[30]

Alan Questel, both an actor trainer and a Feldenkrais practitioner, connects this work on sensitivity to ourselves with the actor's presence. He observes, 'The ability to fill a space so that an actor is seen and heard by the audience and other actors comes naturally to some, but can be developed by all of us. Through the Feldenkrais Method, we can learn to more fully inhabit ourselves in a sensory way.' Questel's notion that actors can learn to 'fully inhabit' themselves 'in a sensory way' brings together the notions of sensing and inhabiting. To explain such 'sensory inhabiting' he claims that 'in doing the Feldenkrais Method, we are practicing our sensations' which involves taking time to 'quietly listen to what we feel and to let the sensation of some of the more unknown parts of ourselves slowly emerge. This results in the ability to feel ourselves more, while expanding our self-image.'[31]

---

[25]Barker 2010: 64.
[26]Barker 2010: 160.
[27]In Foster 1976: 23.
[28]See McCaw 2018: 167.
[29]In Potter 2012: 27.
[30]McConachie and Hart 2006: 5, see also McConachie 2013: 15, Blair 2008: 14.
[31]In Potter 2012: 59.

The phrase 'we are practicing our sensations' articulates perfectly what I mean by sensitivity being an active state that can be developed through training.

Questel's notion of 'expanding our self-image' echoes dancer Dan Wagoner's description of how dancers try 'to find that inward self-image, that kinaesthetic thing of knowing, awareness, simply physical awareness, [which] then begins to feed back and give some kind of image and feeling of *who* you are and *what* you are'. This is the struggle of 'every dancer who is intelligently interested in what they are doing', and you can sense it in some dancers 'in the way they move; you can't think why your eyes go to them, but it's probably for the reason that they have this tremendously strong self-image'.[32] Yet again the connection is being made between a performer becoming more present, more watchable and their active awareness of themselves in motion. They have an image of themselves in movement.

Nontheatrical Accounts of Sensing

Edelman and Tononi echo Lecoq and Barthes when they put the case for how people should be encouraged to develop their senses: 'until we gather sufficient experience, different wines taste more or less the same. But soon, their taste will become associated with strikingly different qualia. Clearly, where there was only the ability to discriminate wine from water, there is now the ability to discriminate reds from whites and Cabernets from Pinots'.[33] This kind of sensory learning is about developing your palate, and the colours of your palette. In their book about the nature and operation of consciousness they explain how we can become conscious of a particular thing precisely because of this skill for discrimination between different qualia. Although we may be considerably slower than computers in calculating, 'we can easily differentiate among billions of different conscious states within a fraction of a second'.[34] Unlike abstract calculation this facility for discriminating between billions of experiences is a feat of real-world thinking.

In Chapter 2 I discussed how the body 'expands' into the world and would argue that the ability to distinguish between the qualities of things forms part of this cognitive expansion. Polyani describes it thus: 'Because our body is involved in the perception of objects, it participates thereby in our knowing of all other things outside. Moreover, we keep expanding our body into the world, by assimilating to it sets of particulars which we integrate into reasonable entities'.[35] This very crisp argument explains an important dimension of embodied knowledge. In two sentences Polyani has sketched how through acts of perception and discrimination we learn to create a world consisting of recognizable things.

---

[32]In Foster 1976: 17–18.
[33]Edelman and Tononi 2000: 174.
[34]Edelman and Tononi 2000: 150.
[35]Polyani 2009: 29.

Feldenkrais similarly uses the words 'discrimination' and 'differentiation' in his account of learning: in *Awareness through Movement* he argues that learning entails 'time, attention, and discrimination', and to discriminate 'we must sense', and such sensing cannot be developed 'by sheer force' of will. He continues, 'More delicate and improved control of movement is possible only through the increase of sensitivity, through a greater ability to sense differences.'[36] Another of his books (1977) documents how he helped a woman (Nora) who had suffered a stroke relearn how to write. He explains how when we learn to write 'we rehearse with constant variations until discrimination occurs.'[37] Andy Clark describes the 'body babbling' of an infant who is learning through self-exploration to recognize which 'neural commands bring about which bodily effects and must practice until skilled enough to issue those commands without conscious effort'. Like Nora (the stroke victim), the infant has to rehearse with constant variations until it can make out successful patterns and strategies, a process that 'continues until the infant body becomes transparent equipment'.[38] (I shall return to phrase 'transparent equipment' below.) Feldenkrais argues, 'Differentiation is discrimination with initiative and is the evidence of the successful process of learning.'[39]

Common to all these arguments is the relation between experience and learning, indeed Feldenkrais argues that *unless* there is a relation between them, we are condemned to repeat our 'old manner of doing'. This in turn prompts Feldenkrais to ask, 'how then is it possible to alter one's behavior to something more satisfactory? The answer is, "by learning"; that is, by forming a new pattern of body configuration and changing the material connected with the mental process.'[40] Feldenkrais's learning is through the body.

What does this more technical discussion add to our understanding of the connection between sensitivity and training? Although the argument has been couched in terms of learning, the outcome is a person who is more expert in making finer judgements and in detecting ever more subtle states of consciousness. There is a double movement in the argument which turns on the double meaning of the word 'sense': the process being described is that of making sense of your sensations, of making meaning from sensation. Understood thus, the sensitivity described by Brook could also be called a certain kind of intelligence. I hope that it is becoming clearer how a human can extend into the world through their acts of perception and learning. I would argue an actor's training also involves (or at least *should* involve) this expanded sensory dimension to its activity.

---

[36]Feldenkrais 1980: 59.
[37]Feldenkrais 1977: 55.
[38]Clark 2011: 34–5.
[39]Feldenkrais 1977: 55.
[40]Feldenkrais 1985: 129–30.

Nontheatrical Accounts of the Kinaesthetic Sense and Proprioception

The Oxford Companion to the Mind defines kinaesthesis as a sense 'which enables us to appreciate the positions and movements of limbs, and depends on receptors in muscles, tendons, and joints, as well as on the sense of muscular effort involved in moving a limb or holding it in a given position'. We also know position and movement from pressure receptors in the bottom of our feet (i.e. our sense of touch). It also explains that movements of the head 'are detected by a set of specialised sense organs in the head, known as the vestibular sense organs', which will be useful when we try to understand the extraordinary case of Ian Waterman who relearned how to walk having lost his senses of both touch and movement. They also explain (among many other things) how sensory and motor systems are coordinated when we reach for an object: 'This requires that sensory spatial information be co-ordinated with the motor commands which control the movements of limbs. This is the process of *sensori-motor co-ordination*.'[41] In rethinking the body as used by the actor we need to incorporate these degrees of complexity. Although the body has to be taken for granted when used instrumentally in performance, we (teachers, practitioners and students) need to create moments of reflection in which we can acknowledge the marvellous complexity and adaptability of our physical selves.

Another term for describing sensory feedback about the body's position (or change of position) is proprioception. A sense of the word comes from its Latin roots, a grasping (*-ception*) of oneself (*proprio-*). This is the self as felt from a first-person perspective: it is *my* body. Gallagher explains, 'Proprioceptive awareness is not itself a perception of the body as an object; for if it were, it would require an ordering system, a spatial frame of reference, that was independent of the body.'[42] His distinction allows us better to understand the distinction between understanding the body from egocentric and allocentric positions. Where Gregory had written about the *sensori-motor* connection, Gallagher points to an intermodal code whereby infants 'already apprehend, with quickly improving precision, the equivalencies between the visible body transformations of others and their own invisible body transformations which they experience proprioceptively'.[43] Whereas as Gibson and Gregory were writing about the relation between self and object, here the sense I have of my own movement informs my understanding of another's movement. As Gallagher puts it: 'From early infancy, then, my visual experience of the other person communicates in a code that is related to the self. What I see of the other's motor behaviour is reflected and played out in terms of my own

---

[41]Gregory 1987: 727.
[42]Gallagher 2005: 137.
[43]Gallagher 2005: 80.

possibilities.'[44] Later in his book Gallagher explains how this sense of my own body provides 'an egocentric frame of reference that is implicitly indexed to the perceiving body, somatic proprioception reflect[ing] the contours of my body, but not from the perspective of another perceiver.'[45] Here he adds another way of rethinking my body: as a framework for grasping the world around me (i.e. in relation to me).

To explain this ability to understand movement Raymond Gibbs introduces the term 'ideomotor action'. Thus, when we see another person 'we do not perceive his or her body as a mere physical thing, but rather as a living body like our own'. Cautiously, he suggests that there 'may be a connection between the mental representation of posture, the movement of one's own body, and perception of posture and movement of other bodies'. He then explains the term 'ideomotor action' which 'refers to body movements that tend to arise in observers as they watch other people perform specific actions.'[46] Much of this paragraph summarizes the perceptuo-sensori-motor activity of mirror neurons.

To conclude this discussion of kinaesthesis and proprioception let us consider the case of a man who retaught himself how to walk despite horrific deficits that followed a viral fever which destroyed sensory nerves throughout his body (leaving him with no sensation below the neck). Ian Waterman's story is documented in Jonathan Coles' *Pride and a Daily Marathon* (1995).[47] I wrote that Waterman 'retaught himself to walk', but this is only partially true. Yes he could walk, but without the sensory feedback from skin and muscles, Waterman had no information about his walking, thus nothing to commit to memory: he could not learn from his movement. As Coles puts it, with 'no way of transferring a newly re-learnt movement from the conscious to the automatic he had to concentrate on each movement each time'. In other words, walking (indeed any anti-gravitational posture other than lying down) demands his total and continuous conscious attention. Coles concludes how skills, once learned, become automatic: 'a skill unconscious, characteristic of the person yet not of their thoughts. Our individuality depends both on our unique ways of walking or writing – unconscious motor skills – and on the quality of our conscious thoughts and behaviour. They are almost indivisible in the eyes of those who meet us. Skills become accepted and so forgotten.'[48] The obvious advantage to making such activities as walking automatic is that it leaves us free to think of other things: 'Ian cannot think of much else when moving.'[49]

---

[44]Gallagher 2005: 81.
[45]Gallagher 2005: 138.
[46]Gibbs 2005: 35.
[47]See also 'The Man Who Lost His Body' (*Horizon*, BBC, 16 October 1997).
[48]Coles 1995: 178.
[49]Coles 1995: 170.

Raymond Gibbs gives the example of a 'simple bodily action like standing up straight' which we have known how to do since infancy. He then talks about how we can fine-tune the posture: 'If our arms are slightly in front of the body, we have to lean back somewhat to compensate for the extra weight in front. If we carry something in front of us, we have to compensate more. The compensating just happens; we don't have to think about it.'[50] Ian Waterman could do none of these things without thinking.

II What Is It That the Body Knows? (What Is Embodied Knowledge?)

Embodied Knowledge

It is precisely because 'embodied knowledge' is such a familiar term that it needs to be defined. Might it simply be about learning? Knowledge that is 'out there' in written and oral form is then embodied – i.e. learned – by an individual. What form does this embodied knowledge (or know-how) take? The first form would be skills such as swimming, driving a car or riding a bicycle. These are very basic motor skills that once learned require little reflection – unless taken to a higher level. Examples in the context of actor training might be such 'skills' as throwing and catching a ball or stick (Exercises 9 and 10 in *Training the Actor's Body*), or simply standing up and sitting down together (Exercise 8). But as I argued in that book the 'training' went far beyond learning the basic skill of throwing and catching balls or sticks. The second form of embodied knowledge consists of techniques that are far more complex than skills; examples would be the specialized knowledge in the fingers of a pastry cook or in those of a Feldenkrais practitioner. They know through their fingers and their knowledge is 'in' their fingers (or rather the neurological connections with their fingers).

We have already encountered the third kind of knowing: discrimination. Edelman and Tononi argued that where humans win out over computers is our ability to discriminate between hundreds of different kinds of wine. Polyani makes a similar observation about how we can recognize a person's face among a 'thousand, indeed among a million. Yet we usually cannot tell how we recognize a face we know. So most of this knowledge cannot be put into words.'[51] With the case of wine-tasting we are dealing with the already-familiar distinction between *savoir* and *saveur* (knowing and savouring); with the face-recognition it is between *savoir* and connaître, that is, between knowing and *recognition,* or in German *wissen* and können. The English word 'knowing' doesn't allow us to make such

---

[50]Gibbs 2005: 29.
[51]Polyani 2009: 4.

distinctions between kinds of knowing. A fourth kind of discriminative knowing is the pattern-recognition that was briefly discussed in Chapter 3 in connection with perception and noticing.

Language: Knowing, Thinking and Learning

One of the paradoxes of this field of practice is that while the learning process often starts with language (in the form of instructions), the actual knowledge (that which is known) cannot easily be rendered verbally. Sennett uses the term 'embedding' to describe 'conversion of information and practices into tacit knowledge' at which point it has become 'so routinized that we don't have to think about it'.[52] Leder uses the example of learning to swim to illustrate that moment of conversion when one no longer needs to think of details like cupping one's hands or breathing and can allow one's 'focus to be directed elsewhere'.[53] The transition is from verbal instruction and consciousness to 'tacit' or embodied knowledge.

Now to discuss the other part of the paradox where 'we know but cannot tell'. Explaining how to tie a slip knot, Sennett argues, would tax 'the powers of the most professional writer'.[54] He goes on to explain that the realm of skill and craftwork lies 'beyond human verbal capacities to explain': 'Here is a, perhaps *the*, fundamental human limit: language is not an adequate "mirror-tool" for the physical movements of the human body'.[55] Sennett has made a powerful case that this realm of activity cannot be understood or accounted for verbally. Claxton makes a similar point when he argues that verbalizing is 'the medium that is most closely tied to normal consciousness' and the one that 'sees' this practical knowledge least well. He echoes Barker's observations on blackberry picking when he argues that when doing something the more '*the self is involved, the more cautious consciousness has to be,* for fear of "getting it wrong"'.[56]

This argument makes some fundamental points about the role language plays in the construction and operation of the self: firstly, that 'normal consciousness' is closely tied to verbalizing, and as a result this 'verbal self' inhibits the successful execution of a task. When a director or trainer encourages an actor or student to 'get out of their heads', I think this is what they mean. A 'head' that offers a running commentary on every activity will get in the way of doing that activity. This explains the advice to 'get out of your own way'. Claxton argues that know-how is 'formatted differently to [language based] knowledge in that it grows by osmosis (rather than comprehension); manifests itself in specific domains of

---

[52]Sennett 2008: 50.
[53]Leder 1990: 31.
[54]Sennett 2008: 95.
[55]Sennett 2008: 95.
[56]Claxton 2000: 120.

expertise (rather than in abstractions); capitalises on serendipity (rather than first principles); and is organised idiosyncratically (rather than systematically)'.[57] This so eloquently describes the more pragmatic learning style of the actor or performer.

When he used the phrase 'normal consciousness' Claxton points to the bias in Western culture to favour knowledge, which is 'normal' over know-how which is less familiar and less respected. Pierre Bourdieu writes of the *scholastic fallacy* which 'induces people to think that agents involved in action, in practice, in life, think, know and see as someone who has the leisure to think thinks, knows and sees'.[58] While there is a place for both types of thinking, knowing and seeing, we must not confuse (or even worse, substitute) one for the other, and should give equal value to both.

Claxton concludes that 'conscious discrimination represents information *that makes a difference*',[59] and although he was writing about a real-world setting, I would argue that the process of actor training is precisely about trying to identify those bits of information that can transform or illuminate one's own practice. However, the meaning of an instruction or advice given in a class might take years to sink in, and then suddenly one day in the studio the penny will drop and you get it. Could one say that at this serendipitous moment the knowledge has become embodied? In this instance there *is* a connection between language and know-how, but the transformation has only been achieved through practice, and only has meaning in the context of that 'specific domain of expertise'. 'Knowing what' can be transmitted and stored easily by printed and electronic media. It is the stuff of academic debate and daily conversation. The knowledge of 'know-how' is much harder won and is registered in the actor's or performer's body.

In the context of developing know-how, what is the difference between a pattern and a habit? Feldenkrais describes 'mature behaviour' (his 1949 book was called *Body and Mature Behaviour*) as 'the capacity of the individual to break up total situations of previous experience into parts, to reform them into a pattern most suitable to the present circumstances'; thus, it is 'an ideal state where the uniqueness of man, his capacity to form new responses, or to learn, has reached its ultimate perfection'.[60] We should note that this behaviour takes place in a real-world situation where value (or meaning) is judged in terms of being 'most suitable to the present circumstances' (in the *Potent Self* he writes about selecting those elements of a movement pattern 'that are expedient for the present moment'[61]). This practice is forward rather than backward moving because the selection is driven by the needs of the present moment. This contrasts with habitual behaviour which

---

[57]Claxton 2000: 41.
[58]Claxton 2000: 41.
[59]Edelman and Tononi 2000: 29–30.
[60]Feldenkrais 2005: 146–7.
[61]Feldenkrais 1985: 44.

simply repeats the already known and learned. An activity becomes habitual (i.e. habitually performed) when we allow it to become so. It is a comfortable groove into which we slip: 'The habitual mode of doing feels right because of repeated approval.'[62] When this happens, our attention is not on the engagement with the present situation. In the context of theatre, this might mean an actor repeating last night's performance, irrespective of the unique rhythms and demands of tonight's audience. Feldenkrais's point gets to the heart of live performance which cannot be a repetition of the already known but must have that element of the unrepeatable here and now. While for him this characterizes maturity of behaviour, it is also central to any creative response to the performance of an activity.

III How Does the Body Learn, Know and Remember?

The Development of Skilled Movement Is Guided by the Senses: Dewey and Bernstein

John Dewey notes how an infant gains knowledge of things – their 'qualities of sound, colour, hardness, etc.' – through the 'activities of handling, reaching, etc., in order to see what results follow upon motor response to a sensory stimulation'. Thus the child learns not 'isolated qualities, but the behaviour which may be expected from a thing, and the changes in things and persons which an activity may be expected to produce'.[63] Here Dewey makes several crucial points: that perception is an activity which involves a whole range of physical movements – 'handling, reaching, etc.' – that take place within a real-world context and which generate sensori-motor loops. Earlier I have stated that sensing is a learned activity, and here we see this learning in action. Handling and reaching are heuristic actions by means of which the child finds out about the world. The knowledge is not simply out there, it is generated through bodily movement, guided by the resulting sensations, and is prompted by a curiosity about the meaning or use of these things for the infant. To acquire a skill a craftsperson must 'have undergone the discipline of experience'.[64] Another word for this 'discipline of experience' is 'practice'.

Well before the flourishing of the neurosciences (his book was published in 1916), Dewey had already sketched out some of the basic principles of learning and movement. He describes the brain as an organ 'for effecting the reciprocal adjustment to each other of the stimuli received from the environment and responses directed upon it'. Furthermore, he includes the dimension of timing

---

[62]Feldenkrais 2005: 109.
[63]Dewey 2004: 260.
[64]Dewey 2004: 252–3.

in this process of mutual interaction, explaining how the brain constantly reorganizes our activity in order to take account of what has 'already been done' and in preparation for 'later acts'. The only way that such monitoring can take place is through an acute sensitivity to the unfolding of the action and the necessary corrections that need to be made. No skill is purely a motor affair.

One of the major contentions of the Soviet neuroscientist Nikolai Bernstein (1896–1966) is that '*there is only one way to make a limb controllable*: From the very onset, the brain must continuously and watchfully check *the movement based on reports of the sensory organs* and harness the movement with corresponding *corrections*.'[65] For example, if one senses that a movement is going too quickly, then the motor response to this sensory feedback is to slow it down. The sensory feedback provokes a motor correction. This establishes the broader principle that a 'motor skill is not a movement formula and certainly not a formula of permanent *muscle forces* imprinted in some motor center. Motor skill is an ability to solve one or another type of motor problem.'[66] A contemporary neurologist, Ramachandran, offers an accessible account of how action and reaction work in the body. Once command signals are sent to the muscles, 'a feedback loop is set in motion. Having received a command to move, the muscles execute the movement. In turn, signals from the muscle spindles and joints are sent back up to the brain, via the spinal cord, informing the cerebellum and parietal lobes that "yes, the command is being performed correctly."'[67]

Bernstein makes a much more obvious connection with theatre training when he observes that the sensory nerves in the muscles and joints increase 'their sensitivity during the practice', which leads him to generalize that in 'each motor skill, *accuracy is undergoing the influence of practice and has a high potential for improvement*'.[68] There is a virtuous loop at work here: as one learns to become more sensitive, so one's practice becomes ever more effective. Consider this in the context of Peter Brook's definition of training as becoming 'quite simply more sensitive'. During the simple exercise of getting up and sitting down (Exercise 8 in *Training the Actor's Body*), all Brook's instructions are concerned with developing a sensory awareness. With such sensory feedback the actor can make ever finer corrections, which often enable them to take away what Feldenkrais calls 'parasitic movements', that is, ones which are unnecessary to the task and which leach one's energy. The generation and understanding of sensory feedback are crucial to the process of learning from one's practice, and by extension the dynamic process of learning how to learn.

The difference between machines and humans, Bernstein observes, is that while the first 'deteriorate with use' it is precisely the opposite with humans: '*The longer*

---

[65]Bernstein 1996: 180.
[66]Bernstein 1996: 181.
[67]Ramachandran 1998: 45.
[68]Bernstein 1996: 216.

a human participates in a certain activity, the *better* he or she performs it. A living organism not only does not deteriorate during work but, quite the opposite, becomes quicker, more enduring and dexterous, particularly with respect to the type of activity that has been performed. This feature of living organisms has been termed *exercisability.*[69] One could call exercisability the ability to learn through the ever-more sensitive exercise of practice. It is the ability to learn how to practise with intelligence. Bernstein's very detailed account of the development of dexterity could almost be used as a model for actor training. Through practice we do not wear ourselves out in the performance of a task, but learn to perform it with ever greater ease.

Bernstein's point that we are not and should not treat ourselves like machines deserves further discussion. In the neuroscientific literature much is made of the plasticity of the brain, indeed this is the main argument of Norman Doidge's book *The Brain That Changes Itself* (2007). When Russian actors talk about physical training they use the word 'plastic' to convey the idea of working on flexibility. We could go further in our rethinking of the actor's body by developing our notion of plasticity. Unlike a machine the body is designed for learning and is changed in the process. A little like Heraclitus saying that you never walk in the same river twice (because the water is never the same), so the body is never the same, since it is in a constant state of cellular regeneration. We are soft machines that are changed by our constant interactions with our environment.

It is the crucial role of sensory feedback that distinguishes humans from machines, and specifically from computers. Thinking of the body as a machine and the brain as a computer is part of everyday culture. A vivid example of this conception can be found in James Cameron's 1984 film *The Terminator.* When Arnold Schwarzenegger's cyborg enters a room, various screens appear in his visual array with estimates of threats: their number, distance and types. This is to suggest that perception is passive, rather than a very active process of sense-making or, as Polyani will describe it below 'interpretation'. Once the scene has been assessed, an appropriate response is calculated and then delivered in a devastating hail of gunfire and ordinance. This model of action has only two stages: perception followed by action, or to use behaviourist terminology stimulus and response. There is no suggestion that the initial movement plan could be subject to correction following sensory feedback. There is no reflection.

What It Is That We Remember?

There are two kinds of memory: *explicit* and *implicit* (or procedural), a division that maps on to knowing *what* – explicit memory splits into semantic memory about events of public record and biographical events – and knowing *how,* i.e. practical

---

[69]Bernstein 1996: 171.

skills. In this chapter, indeed in this book, we are dealing with implicit and not explicit memory. A major misconception (again rendering us as machines) is that a memory is some kind of facsimile, stored as an image or sound in the brain (or body) and then retrieved intact like a book from a library. If Bernstein is correct, then a memory is not likely to be a muscular engram of an action.

Alain Berthoz introduces the notion of 'motor equivalence' to argue that we do not memorize intentional actions as muscular patterns. He writes of a kind of memory whose output 'can be used to make a move using different effectors' and gives the example of 'a letter using a finger, hand, or foot. Very few current models include this property of motor equivalence.'[70] In other words, the same memory of a move can be effected using different part of the body (hence the term 'motor equivalence'). Alex Kozulin elaborates this point using the same example, arguing that if writing our name were a muscular habit 'then every new posture of a subject would require the establishment of a whole new system of muscular regulations. However, the uniformity – that is, the equal simplicity – of writing in different postures indicates that the central formula of this habit is not connected to a particular muscular organization. The engrams of the habit resemble a final good – personal handwriting – rather than a muscular skill.'[71]

The argument of Berthoz and Kozulin bears out Bernstein's claim that physical learning is not about acquiring motor skills. But the notion of 'motor equivalence' goes further than his idea of sensori-motor integration, since it suggests that the common factor in all these different muscular regulations is what Kozulin calls a 'central formula', or 'final good'. The physical effector patterns (i.e. different ways of doing) are all variables, whereas the constant is this always-similar pattern that is common to all the physical iterations. 'Writing your name in Space' (Exercise 56 in *Training the Actor's Body*) offers a practical exploration of this theme.

Learning and the Disappearing Body

I hinted in Chapter 1 that our bodies are instruments of learning, a capacity that can be developed through continuous training. In looking at learning through this lens we find another paradox: as one learns, so the body, or indeed the tools that the body uses to learn disappear. Polyani explains that as we learn 'to use a stick for feeling our way, our awareness of its impact on our hand is transformed into a sense of its point touching the objects we are exploring'. This becomes a process whereby the touching of the object transposes 'meaningless feelings into meaningful ones'. Through what he calls 'an interpretative effort' we 'become aware of the feelings in our hand in terms of their meaning located at the tip of the probe or stick to which we are attending'.[72]

---

[70]Berthoz 2000: 213.
[71]Kozulin 1984: 67.
[72]Polyani 2009: 12–13.

This dynamic engagement marks a double learning process, about the capacity of hand movements to generate meaning, and thereby to learn about the nature of the object. But it also describes how (to return to Clark's notion of the extended body) we can learn to incorporate the instrument 'in our body – or extend our body to include it – so that we come to dwell in it'.[73,74] This progressive forgetting of the arm and stick as we learn to focus on the object leads Polyani to state that our body is the only thing 'we normally never experience as an object', since our attention is directed from our body (call it our centre) outwards to the world. In our interactions with the world the body becomes a means and not an object of knowing. Clark borrows Heidegger's phrase 'transparent equipment' to describe how our body is 'not the focus of attention', nor even the tools we use, rather the 'user "sees through" the equipment to the task in hand'.[75]

When a skill is finally and fully learned, it comes, as Leder puts it, 'to pervade my own corporeality', it 'has been incorporated into my bodily "I can"'.[76] He calls this process of learning and remembering 'something akin to a sedimentary process': 'Over time, that which is acted out, rehearsed and repeated seeps into one's organismic ground'.[77] We saw above how this process of repetition and rehearsal begins with an 'I can' (self-acknowledgement of the skill) and finally 'contracts into the "I do," that region of body possibility that I actually use'. The problem comes when he notes that 'because of the nature of incorporation, is it not easy to excise or even recognise such habits'. The skill simply disappears from view and becomes 'enveloped within the structure of the taken-for-granted body from which I in*habit* the world'.[78]

There are two problems with this argument. The first is a failure to distinguish between two kinds of movement: those that are 'exploratory' (the stick as a sensing device), and those that are 'performatory' (when the stick is used to hit something). This was a distinction made by James Gibson.[79] My second concern is the suggestion that such a form of learning is little more than the acquisition of a habit. There is a difference between a skill which simply disappears from view and tacit knowledge (where one knows but simply cannot tell). The question lies in the state of attentiveness, that is, the degree to which one remains aware of one's learned movements and thus can change them to address the specifics of the immediate situation; the alternative to this adaptability or exercisability (Bernstein's term used above) is habitual repetition.

Edelman and Tononi take the far more complex example of learning the piano (a question of technique and not skill) where the first steps are laborious

---

[73] Polyani 2009: 16.
[74] Merleau-Ponty (1962: 151–2) makes a very similar point about how a blind person uses their cane.
[75] Clark 2011: 10.
[76] Leder 1990: 31.
[77] Leder 1990: 32.
[78] Leder 1990: 32.
[79] Gibson 1968: 45–6.

and prone to error, precisely because it is being controlled at every step by our conscious mind. They develop Claxton's argument about how the conscious self can inhibit and impede learning movement. They ascribe a student's awkwardness to the fact that they use 'the whole hand, the forearm and even the entire body, especially the head' rather than refining the movement to simply the fingers. It takes years of practice to reach the state when the impulse to play a note 'effects the contraction of a few limited muscles'.[80] Feldenkrais would say that at this optimal stage the practitioner has learned how to remove all superfluous movement and effort. Through repeated practice conscious control becomes 'superfluous and disappears' until the pianist can let a 'scale rattle itself off at great speed'.[81] Again, I would argue such a 'rattling off' of scales is a purely mechanical technique. An interpretative artist does more than 'rattle off' pieces of music.

Sennett offers a more nuanced account of the higher stages of a skill where 'there is a constant interplay between tacit knowledge and self-conscious awareness, the tacit knowledge serving as an anchor, the explicit awareness serving as critique and corrective. Craft quality emerges from this higher stage, in judgments made on tacit habits and suppositions'.[82] I would add that in this awareness lies the creativity of the interpretative artist, be they pianist or actor. Gallagher makes a similar turn in his argument. Like other commentators he begins by noting how 'Smooth movement, successful walking, reaching and grasping depend on a certain experiential transparency of the body'. This is because 'movement usually takes care of itself'. But then he introduces a kind of awareness that he calls 'a pre-reflective, performative awareness rather than a vivid perceptual presence'.[83] The point is that in order for an actor to give a 'live' rather than a repeated performance they need a certain double state of attentiveness. One can describe this as a 'constant interplay between tacit knowledge and self-conscious awareness' or a 'pre-reflective, performative awareness', the main point is that there is an awareness, a sensitivity, to how a series of learned movements are being performed.

Paradoxes of Knowing and Telling

I have identified a number of paradoxes surrounding the process of learning or the incorporation of movement skills, the biggest of which is that in order for a skill to be performed fluently (with flow) the performer has to be able to do it *without thinking*. Thus, although one learns how to do it, once learned, once embodied, this skill becomes tacit – silent. This prompts important questions about teaching and learning. Is the learning of a skill a once-and-forever event that happens at the

---

[80]William James in Edelman and Tononi 2000: 59.
[81]Edelman and Tononi 2000: 57.
[82]Sennett 2008: 50.
[83]Gallagher 2005: 91.

beginning of one's career? Or if, as Stanislavsky has suggested, training is a continual process, then how does one re-connect with a skill? Maybe the whole problem lies in the words 'skill' and 'technique': if the aim of training is to become 'quite simply more sensitive', then it could be conceived as an open-ended process. Maybe we should stop talking about knowledge (stuff acquired) and adopt Bernstein's notion of dexterity being about problem-solving. This connects with Feldenkrais's idea that mature behaviour consists in being able to breaking up learned patterns of behaviour and adapting them to novel situations; in other words, another kind of problem-solving. All of which suggests that we should be talking about developing a bodily form of intelligence, rather than acquiring motor skills. This intelligence is fed by a particular kind of mental, attentional energy which should accompany the performance of an action. The performer needs to have what Gallagher above called a 'pre-reflective, performative awareness' which is different to that 'self-conscious' awareness which inhibits spontaneous movement.

We must be careful in transposing theories predicated on real-world behaviour onto what happens on a stage. In a stage performance an actor is not performing an action, but creating an image of someone performing an action in a particular way. A 'character' is known through their particular and recognizable ways of doing. The content of a task in theatre is less important than the manner of its execution. Interpretative know-how places the emphasis upon the 'how'. This explains why an actor has to develop a sensitivity to the full spectrum of movement qualities, that is, of how other humans move. Actors operate in two times, two spaces and, in a way, two bodies: the fictional time and space of the play and the body of the character as well as the actual time and space of the performance and their own bodies. They have to be aware of the actual form of the performance, its rhythms of time and space. Where Sennett has written about craft I would suggest that we are here dealing with artistry. To sustain this artistry requires the self-knowledge (again, not necessarily verbal or conscious) that comes through continuing training and development.

Summary

Inside/Outside – Egocentric/Allocentric Perspectives

Although the theme of inside/outside might at first sight seem a throwback to dualist thought, it is actually the site of an extremely complex knot of problems concerning how living organisms interact with their environment. This knot consists of relations between subject and subject (as moving beings we understand the movements of other moving beings), subject and object (our sensory discrimination of qualia), of spatial perspectives (ego- and allocentric), of the 'incorporation' or 'inhabiting' of skills.

Paradoxes of Learning

This process itself has generated a set of paradoxes about learning: through the process of *in*habiting a skill, we both know and do not know how we do it. In order to perform an action fluently we have to be able to do it without thinking. I have argued that an actor has to have a specialized form of attention whereby they can maintain a residual if non-conscious awareness of the movements they perform. Just as an actor cannot perform habitually (as themselves) so they cannot act mechanically (automatically). Bernstein has explained why a human is not a machine, and why we do not have muscle memory. Like Brook he argues training is a process of progressive sensitization, a dynamic and continuing process, not a once-only establishment of a habit. Once again, we must appreciate the value of time as a dimension of learning and training.

Being in Your Body: Are There Degrees of Being in Your Body?

Returning to the question of attention raised in Chapter 3 we can now grasp that alongside mental attention (the direction of consciousness), there is a bodily state of awareness, or soft focus, whereby an actor can monitor their performance. We can be 'in our body' (i.e. attentive to its every movement) or 'in our head' (a state of verbal reflection where we are not attending to the immediate sensory feedback from our body). The actor's task is to find an attentional state that allows them both to perform and to be aware of the process of that performance.

The question of 'being in the body' suggests a dualism of mind and body, of inner and outer, against which I have argued throughout this chapter. If we can talk about our body being absent or transparent in its action, our brain is even more so in its exquisitely complex operations. We may not know how the brain creates the mind, but I side with those neuroscientists who argue that we are one single organism operating without a central controller in our head. We are all body. Our process operates without a programme.

How Do We Know Our Own Bodies?

Our proprioceptive sense is actually a mixture of different senses. We saw the tragic consequences of losing proprioception in the case of Ian Waterman for whom even the simple act of standing still requires immense conscious effort. Essential though it is, this knowledge of ourselves is rarely foregrounded in our consciousness, indeed much of it is inaccessible to consciousness.

Drew Leder argues that during the performance of an action our attention is on the object of our task and not on our body, which he describes as being 'absent'. Others describe the body becoming transparent when used as an instrument.

When we use instruments (be it a hammer or a visually impaired person's stick) they become incorporated into our transparent, tacit body. An actor needs to maintain a degree of awareness of their body in performance, since it is not being used as an instrument but as an image.

How Do We Know through Our Bodies?

Through learning to make sense of our bodily sensations we render sensation into information. We 'know' one wine from another through developing a more discerning palate. Although we cannot compare with a computer in terms of computational capacity, our ability to distinguish between billions of conscious states far outstrips any machine.

Brook argues that the aim of performer training is to develop sensitivity. Bernstein argues that the way to learn skills is through sensitivity. Our bodies cannot be programmed like machines but need to learn from how we perform actions, or as Feldenkrais put it, we learn by developing our awareness through movement.

PART TWO

5 A PRESENT BODY

Introduction: The Connection between Presence and Energy

How is it that an actor can stand on stage and hold an audience's attention without speaking or moving? An actor is uniquely trained to have an effect on the audience through their physical presence alone. Do actors with this presence have a special kind of energy? Is this energy related to that mentioned in Asian martial arts which propose that the body's health and effective movement are maintained by the circulation of vital energy, which is in part generated through breathing? This energy – variously called *chi* (Chinese), *ki* (Japanese) or *prana* (Sanskrit) – courses through channels in the body and is gathered in particular centres. Of all chapters in this book this one may seem to have the least resonance for the scientific community since it deals with a conception of the human body that is based on a community of experience and practice rather than any objective evidence. However, there are points of contact (questions of attention, awareness and sensitivity) not least the connection I make between energy and what psychologist Daniel Stern (2010) calls forms of vitality. My hope is to make sense of this fundamental aspect of the actor's body and in doing so offer a bridge to a more scientific study.

An actor's body is 'present' in two senses of the word: it is there in time present and is physically present in space; it is also presented for an audience to look upon (*theatron* in ancient Greek was 'a place to look upon'). Although presence is certainly something associated with stage and screen, it is also an everyday phenomenon: there are certain people who seem to light up a room when they enter. Having worked with a number of actors over the years I have noticed that while they have an incandescent presence onstage, offstage they can be utterly unnoticeable. Is presence therefore something that can be turned on and off? Can it be developed or is it innate? These are questions I had to consider when writing a chapter on presence for Mark Evans' *The Actor's Training Reader* (2015). It opened with a recollection of my years auditioning and waiting for the 'right' actor to put their head around the door.

It was always a case of 'the minute you walked through the door': some actors just had 'it', whatever 'it' is, and it was immediately apparent. Let us say for the moment that it was a certain quality of presence – they were just more 'there', more 'now', their reaction to the space and to us was quicker and more alive than the others. I never recall an actor gradually becoming present after their entrance had been a non-event. Guiltily, I once asked a friend, the late John McGrath (writer and director for film and stage), whether he had the same experience. Absolutely, he replied.[1]

I have done no extensive survey, but I feel sure that this 'the moment you walked through the door' is a recognized phenomenon, and it concerns presence.

The article then turned to an experience later in my career when I was artistic director of the International Workshop Festival. I had inherited a collaboration with London's South Bank Centre, and I was searching for a theme that would unite the different elements of the festival (workshops, talks, presentations and a performance). The answer was presence.

The project was called *The Performer's Energy*, and, by some strange synchronicity, a few months later [1996] Eugenio Barba's ISTA (International School for Theatre Anthropology) was organising a project called *The Performer's Bios*. We both agreed that energy or *bios* was an essential element in the performer's presence. It is the vital energy that seems to light up the actor from within, that gives them power on stage, that sets them more presently before us. If Eugenio and I were organising practical workshops for performers around the questions of energy and presence, you can infer that we both felt that these can be developed through training.[2]

Although I pinned my colours to the mast in this article and stated my belief in there being such a thing as the performer's energy, I have to admit that, over twenty years on, I am still no closer to being able to explain what exactly it is.

Energy Pro and Contra: Feldenkrais and the Martial Arts

In the last chapter Feldenkrais practitioner and actor-trainer Alan Questel accounted for an actor's presence in terms of sensory awareness. This in turn is a result of a sense of embodiment; when embodied 'we could say that we are more connected to ourselves; we know what we are feeling, and we can feel ourselves

---

[1]McCaw 2015: 169.
[2]McCaw 2015: 169.

more'.[3] Questel reaffirms the value of having a whole or connected body, a principle that is espoused by all trainings I've come across. Questel suggests that awareness of oneself is another way of saying of being present to oneself. He defines 'presence' in terms of occupancy; an actor who is present can 'fill a space' and thus be 'seen and heard by the audience'. Just as one talks of vocal projection, is Questel here suggesting a kind of bodily projection? He goes on to argue that this ability comes naturally to some, it 'can be developed by all of us'. How? By learning 'to more fully inhabit ourselves in a sensory way', and in developing this 'ability to feel ourselves more' we are also 'expanding our self-image'.[4]

Mia Segal, one of Feldenkrais's earliest disciples, notes that 'every part of your body should participate' in every movement you make. Feldenkrais would argue

that even your little toe should know what the head is doing and enhance that activity. Even if you cannot see the movement of the little toe, there should be no interference from it. Those parts of you which are unaware that there is movement are interfering with your movement – not assisting it. How do you keep the various parts from interfering? By becoming aware that you have these areas.[5]

Certainly the Feldenkrais Method can help students (be they actors or not) become more aware of themselves through how they move. In this sense they have expanded their personal image of themselves. It remains an open question whether an actor who has expanded their self-image will thereby have expanded their image in the eyes of the spectator. That is one aspect of Feldenkrais's account of an actor's presence. We will now see that he in no way subscribed to the association of presence with energy.

In his biography Mark Reece noted how Moshe Feldenkrais was critical when people used the term 'energy' to 'express immeasurable phenomena or to label experiences that people had trouble describing' and impatient when someone 'invoked energy in pseudoscientific "explanations" that masked a lack of understanding'. Feldenkrais would urge 'scepticism and scientific discourse'.[6] The issue only arose because, apart from being a research scientist, he was also practised in the martial arts and studied Judo under disciples of Master Jigoro Kano (1860–1938), its founder. During these studies he would most certainly have come across the notion that *ki* is gathered in an area called the *tanden* just beneath and behind the navel. In an interview with Dani Leiri on the martial arts Feldenkrais declares that he has no connection with these 'sorts of metaphysical meanings and powers', going on to describe 'the concept of ki and *chi* as an incredible impediment to

---

[3]Questel in Potter 2012: 59.
[4]Questel in Potter 2012: 59.
[5]Segal in Johnson 1995: 115.
[6]Reece 2015: 117.

learning'. Just as tersely he states that 'the idea of *chi* or *ki* is preposterous'. The quotation continues:

> What can you do with it? What change will it make to you? Now, it sounds a mysterious kind of super power that you get from somewhere in the point in your stomach, and that point described properly [i.e. the *tanden*], is the duodenum lying there and is literally full of shit.[7]

Even allowing for Feldenkrais's delight in upsetting apple carts, this is an unusually (unnecessarily?) vehement and unambiguous rejection of the notion of energy. While I do not share Feldenkrais's total dismissal of the possible existence of this energy, I share his unease with how often and how vaguely the term is used.

A quite different perspective on energy is offered by A.C. Scott, a scholar of Japanese and Chinese theatre, and creator of the Asian Theatre Program at the University of Wisconsin-Madison. Scott defines *tai chi* as a 'discipline devised to attain and retain balance through an ability to conserve and direct physical energy, not to squander it'. At the very least Feldenkrais and Scott would agree on the value of energy conservation. I would further argue that stillness comes from the direction and control of one's energy resource. Scott notes that the study of tai chi 'demands patience, perseverance, and concentration – the latter undoubtedly a vital benefit it confers on students of acting'.[8] This explains why his actor training was based on regular sessions of tai chi.

> It was made clear to the students that the exercises were primarily aimed at improving their sense of physical control and powers of concentration in the limited time available for the work we had to do on stage, and that a really thorough command of *t'ai chi ch'uan* was a long-term involvement. Nevertheless, as we slowly progressed it was gratifying to find a perceptible improvement in control, timing and restraint.[9]

Scott confines his argument to very practical considerations of acting (indeed of effective action-taking). Tai chi improves physical control, powers of concentration and timing to which he adds a 'sensitivity to the dramatic function of silence',[10] 'a greater sense of their physical potential as actors [and] a better realisation of their bad habits'.[11] Recognizing one's bad habits is another form of self-awareness and, as we've already seen, a central aspect of the Feldenkrais Method.

---

[7]Feldenkrais 1986: 12.
[8]Scott 1993: 51.
[9]Scott 1993: 53.
[10]Scott 1993: 54.
[11]Scott 1993: 55.

Scott concludes with a very sophisticated observation about how an awareness of one's body in action leads to a particular form of readiness. He explains how the relation between the performer and their body 'becomes manifest in the process of articulation, which stimulates awareness of the anticipatory moment preceding change – what Jacques Copeau so tellingly described as "that expressive stillness which contains the embryo of the action to follow."'[12] This densely but very precisely worded observation deserves further comment. There is a connection between how the relation between the performer and their body can *become manifest* and Questel's notion of how an actor can develop their self-image. The 'anticipatory moment preceding change' is a phrase that Feldenkrais could have used as it describes that moment of suspension before movement, a moment of awareness of the movement to come. For Feldenkrais it is in this moment of awareness in which learning takes place. Although Feldenkrais and Scott might have different opinions about energy, there is much common ground in their definitions of intelligent movement.

Being There Just by Standing Still

Copeau's evocation of 'that expressive stillness which contains the embryo of the action to follow' returns us to the image with which this chapter opened.

> An actor stands absolutely still in front of an audience, not moving a muscle rendering an expression, nor uttering a sound, yet affecting the spectator to tears or laughter.[13]

Although not posed as a question, this brief description of an actor's work does make one think 'How do they do it?' And if the answer were that the actor is simply being present, then I would, once more, repeat the question 'How?' Elaborating on this conundrum about stillness and presence in his preface to *The Paper Canoe* (1993), Eugenio Barba asks the same question about stillness and presence: 'Can a performer who does not move hold the spectator's attention?' Subsequent questions hint at an answer:

> What is the performer's presence? Why, when two performers execute the same actions, is one believable and the other not? [...] Of what does energy in the theatre consist?[14]

---

[12]Scott 1993: 55–6.
[13]Zinder 2009: xi.
[14]Barba 1993: ix (see also Barba and Savarese 1991: 10).

Scott offers his own variation on this question of how an actor can move an audience without making a movement: they must achieve the task of 'standing still while not standing still'.[15] This is actually an instruction from tai chi where the student is reminded of the tai chi symbol where in the emptiness there is always a small and crucial element of fullness and vice versa. When the discussion turns to Stanislavsky, we will see that even when sitting still an actor still needs to be active (something needs to be going on inside them).

Scott also insists that 'a silent actor must still remain a physical presence on the stage'.[16] While the question of stillness and presence might remain a conundrum, this question is at the heart of all acting, be it in the realist tradition or post-dramatic. An actor has to be 'in character' before they speak a line. This is more a question of technique than mystique.

Zarrilli makes a connection with the actor training proposed by Jacques Copeau who

> wanted to develop a form of training the actor which was not that of the athlete for whom the body remains an instrument or tool. He wanted a training through which 'normally developed bodies [become] capable of adjusting themselves, *giving themselves over* to any action they may undertake.' It is a

FIGURE 5.1 The Tai Chi *Yin-Yan* Symbol.

---

[15]Scott cited in http://www.phillipzarrilli.com/trainapp/index1.html (accessed 10 August 2016).
[16]In Zarrilli 2009: 25.

state in which the actor has mastered motionlessness and is *ready* for what comes next.[17]

This echoes Copeau's notion of 'expressive stillness' and establishes the relation between a mastery of motionlessness with the state of readiness: stillness is not inactivity but a preparedness to act. Here one can see connections with Peter Brook's exercise of standing up and sitting down[18] (which, I have already noted, owes a great deal to Feldenkrais's teaching), and also with the discussion about states of attentiveness. A quotation from Copeau himself brings us back to the theme of stillness:

> An actor without skills find stillness very difficult … such a technique implies a prepared, breathing, concentrated actor, with clear intentions, permitting the action to be sustained in the inaction. Stillness commands great power and authority in the theatre space. An actor must learn how to use it.[19]

It would seem that the *skill* of being still marks out the mature from the student actor. Returning to my opening questions, an actor's ability to be there whilst still would appear to be about developing a sensitivity to both time and space which explains why Scott placed so much emphasis on an actor learning about timing. This is quite as much about technique as it is energy. It is about the potentiality of that moment before action. Even though the actor has not done anything, their presence is immensely powerful because we know they are about to do something and we don't know what. This capacity for action is dangerous and exciting. For me, the most vivid example of this dangerous potentiality was Alun Armstrong as Barabas the Jew in the RSC's 1987 production of *The Jew of Malta*. As he prowled through the audience he was terrifying precisely because he was so unpredictable. One didn't know what he was going to do next. He was like an unexploded bomb.

Returning to the first quotation from Scott above, perhaps now it is possible to understand how an actor can achieve the required concentration span and thus achieve 'directness, simplicity and intensity' in their performance. In his article 'Exercises' Grotowski recalls Stanislavsky's observations of his cat who is never in a state of total relaxation, 'This means that his muscles actually mobilise up to the necessary point and no more.'[20] In tai chi one would express this state of

---

[17]Zarrilli 2009: 25.

[18]In McCaw 2018: Exercise 8.

[19]In Potter 2012: 28.

[20]Grotowski 1979: np. The passage referred to is on page 126 of *The Actor's Work* (2008b) where Kostya [the young Stanislavsky] watches a cat move from a number of positions 'upside down, on his side, on his back!' 'And in each of these positions you could observe him tense for the first second and immediately relaxing with extraordinary ease, get rid of the unnecessary and fix the necessary tension.'

ready-resting as being 'relaxed but not yet relaxed'. All the master pedagogues quoted (Copeau, Grotowski, Stanislavsky) all agree on the need for the actor to shed all excess and un-productive tension and thus achieve a sense of potentiality and readiness. Here we have a non-mystical account of presence on which all the commentators so far mentioned would agree.

The Pneumatic and the Hydraulic Body

Chapter 2 of Joseph Roach's *The Player's Passion* (1993) is called 'Nature Still, but Nature Mechanised'. His fascinating study invites us to rethink the actor's body by considering historically earlier patterns of knowledge. If we fail to address these patterns with sympathetic imagination, then we will not understand earlier – in this instance, David Garrick's – approaches to acting. Key to understanding Garrick's approach to acting – and to the actor's body – was La Mettrie's *L'homme machine* (1747) which explained how the human body was moved by hydraulic forces in the same way to those that animated the automata which were so popular at the time. Roach describes how Descartes 'seized upon such automata as the functional analogies of the human body and nervous system'[21] and how water acted the part of a spring 'in a double sense: as a reservoir and as a medium of propulsion'.[22] The human body is conceived as a 'terrestrial machine' that is hydraulically powered. Roach's description deserves quoting in full:

> When the spring is pushed, the machine stirs. The 'rational soul' pushes on a gland in the center of the brain, and the nerves, which resemble hollow tubes, convey this pressure by a subtle fluid or current called animal spirits. The 'will' or the 'imagination', both functions of the soul, presses the gland, which presses the muscles throughout the entire body and makes them swell and contract as needed – in very much the same manner as that of an hydraulic brake system in an automobile.[23]

Although Roach argues that this notion of the *homme machine* 'confronts today's reader with a recondite physiological paradigm'[24] I would suggest that its image of the hydraulic person is uncannily similar to the notion of vital energy circulating throughout the body. While Feldenkrais might reject this notion with scatological vehemence, it is most certainly part of contemporary discussion in both the performing and the martial arts.

---

[21]Roach 1993: 62.
[22]Roach 1993: 62.
[23]Roach 1993: 63.
[24]Roach 1993: 68.

Before returning the discussion of the circulation of energy in the context of actor training, I want to make a further connection with contemporary thinking. Psychologist Daniel Stern notes how Freud uses this same image of hydrodynamics when he writes of psychic energy flowing, welling up and subsiding: 'All these notions are in the prevailing metaphoric language of hydrodynamics. At times, this hydrodynamic model was only metaphoric, while at other times it was reified and used as explanatory.'[25] I shall return to Stern's *Forms of Vitality* (2010) at the end of this chapter to argue that states of energy (and therefore presence) can be understood as *forms of vitality*.

In the literature on actor training there are two dominant metaphors used to describe the circulation of energy in the actor's body: circulation and blockage. The direction of flow is almost always from the centre outwards to the periphery. Terry Schreiber offers a useful illustration:

> Human bodies are filled with energy. [...] Whatever it's called, the basic idea is the same: Human bodies have energy flowing through them, from the crown of the head to the tips of the toes. And like water in a garden hose, the energy flows freely when there are no kinks of tension blocking its way.[26]

Using the image of garden hose Schreiber argues that energy flows throughout the actor's body and that tension blocks this circulation. For St Denis whatever his students do on stage, and no matter how small the gesture, 'a kind of current, *life,* must go through the *whole* body. He will gradually discover that his entire body takes part in the gesture even if it does not move with it.'[27] This notion of unhindered circulation of vital energy provides a model for understanding how the whole body is involved in any and every movement. According to St Denis the 'originating motor of movement should be in the centre of the body, from which all movement passes to the extremities, creating a continuous flow'. He concludes by warning that if a movement 'is done mechanically, it does not leave anything behind it; it has no more effect on an actor's expressiveness than water running through a tap'.[28] Could one see in this vector of energy from centre to periphery a metaphor for intention whereby the meaning (or expressiveness) of the movement is the result of the *direction* of the actor's energy? This directedness is what contrasts with a purely mechanical execution of the movement. The paradox of this conception of human vitality is that while it argues against a mechanical approach to movement, it relies on there being an 'originating motor' to get the energy into circulation. Although Roach worries that a reference to La Mettrie's

---

[25]Stern 2010: 34
[26]Schreiber 2005: 7.
[27]St Denis 1982: 104.
[28]St Denis 1982: 104.

homme machine might be recondite, it is clear that this model of the actor's body is still in current use.

The principle metaphors at work in this section are as follows:

- In order to promote the unimpeded flow of vital energy an actor needs to be free of (muscular) tension, to be open and flexible. (The theme of blocking and flowing.)

- A body without tensions can participate *as a whole* in a movement, no matter how small. (The theme of part and whole.)

- Energy is generated in the 'centre' of the body and finds expression in the periphery; its outward flow can be given direction and this is what invests a movement with meaning. (The themes of inner and outer, and the new theme of direction of energy = the meaning of a movement.)

Stanislavsky, Yoga and *Prana*

We began with the image of an actor on stage neither moving nor speaking and yet still capable of holding the audience's attention. In his autobiography Stanislavsky questions whether there are any actors who possess such an ability. 'Oh, if only there were actors capable of carrying out a simple piece of staging, such as standing by the prompter's box. How much simpler it would make our work. But such actors do not exist.'[29] In his researches he 'observed great actors' to judge how long they could hold the audience's attention while doing almost nothing, and it ranged from a minimum of one minute to a maximum of seven minutes.[30] Stanislavsky returns to the subject in *An Actor's Work* where the students are asked to sit onstage without moving. They all find it hard not to fidget, finding it easier to 'sit onstage in a theatrical rather than a human way – unnaturally'.[31] When none of the student actors can achieve the task, Tortsov (a character modelled on the older Stanislavsky) demonstrates how to sit onstage without doing anything, that is, without *feeling the need to do something*. (An example of stage behaviour that is driven by the conscious mind.) His students note that 'the simple way he sat captured our attention'.[32] He managed to hold their attention because his stillness had an intention behind it: 'Everything that happens onstage must occur for *some reason or other*'.[33] Once again, meaning (i.e. believability) is associated with intention, with having a reason for performing one's actions. Tortsov continues by saying that 'physical stillness is the result of intense inner action, and that is

---

[29]Stanislavsky 2008a: 156.
[30]Stanislavsky 2008a: 156.
[31]Stanislavsky 2008b: 38.
[32]Stanislavsky 2008b: 39.
[33]Stanislavsky 2008b: 39.

especially important and interesting in creative work' which leads him to propose a refinement of his earlier definition of theatre as action: 'action is action – mental and physical.'[34]

This redefinition of 'action' is crucial: it is not simply about physical but also mental activity. Stanislavsky, Copeau, Barba, Zinder and Zarrilli all agree that although it seems a contradiction, to be still on stage requires a certain kind of activity, and as St Denis adds, it also requires training and performance experience. Where others have written about how tension blocks the flow of energy, Stanislavsky touches on the source of this muscular tension: stage fright or anxiety. He also suggests that actors feel constrained to do something rather than simply being there 'naturally', taking us back to his sustained critique of theatricality (most often this means the early theatre of Meyerhold). There is a saying attributed to both Peter Ustinov and Ronald Reagan: 'Don't just do something, stand there.' It is not as easy as it seems. We have to discipline what is going on in our heads. Rather than allowing a constant stream of thoughts about what one should be doing, maybe an actor should just focus on what they are actually doing and how this matches with what is happening around them.

Stanislavsky was perhaps one of the first director/pedagogues to connect an actor's onstage presence with their state of energy and took much inspiration from yoga. According to Hulton and Kapsali (2015), Stanislavsky read the books on yoga by 'Ramachakara' (the *nom de plume* of an American lawyer called William Walker Atkinson (1862–1932)). They write of 'the striking similarities between the writings of the two men'[35]: for example, their mutual interest in the connection between vital energy (*prana*) and breathing, the superconscious (a state of transcendence) and states of attention and concentration, relaxation (which they argue is both a mental *and* a physical state). This leads them to connect his principle of purposeful action 'which encapsulates a sense of body-mind integration absolutely in tune with the practice of yoga postures as they have been developed within contemporary practice'.[36] This discussion of purposeful action brings us back to the theme of intention and of its projection from the centre to the periphery. To borrow a term from Stanislavsky's student Michael Chekhov, this is a state of 'radiation'.[37]

Chapter 10 of *The Actor's Work* is titled 'Communication' and features a reflection on the communicative effect of radiation. Tortsov wonders aloud whether his students have ever 'been aware, in life or onstage, when in communication with other people, of a current emanating from your will, flowing through your eyes, your fingertips, your skin'. He wonders what to call this method of communication:

---

[34]Stanislavsky 2008b: 40.
[35]Hulton and Kapsali 2015: 10.
[36]Hulton and Kapsali 2015: 13.
[37]Chekhov 1985: 16, 147, 153; Chekhov 1991: 32, 46–8, 137.

'*Emitting and receiving rays, signals? Radiating out* and *radiating in*? […] In the near future, when this invisible current has been studied by science, a more appropriate terminology will be established.'[38] I wonder if the latter sentence was included to appease the Soviet censors who most certainly would have been dubious about such a concept. Stanislavsky appears to have been pragmatic about the concept of *prana.*

> I have no desire to prove whether Prana really exists or not. My sensations may be purely individual to me, the whole thing may be the fruit of my imagination. This is all of no consequence provided I can make use of it for my purposes and it helps me. If my practical and unscientific method can be of use to you, so much the better. If not, I shall not insist on it.[39]

This is another example of the actor's pragmatism regarding method; an approach is valued because it works for them personally, and this their only criterion.

Many writers have discussed the connection between Stanislavsky and yoga. Leopold Sulerzhitsky (1872–1916) introduced Stanislavsky to yoga,[40] and Vera Soloviova, a member of his First Studio, recalls how they worked a great deal on 'concentration'. 'We imagined a circle around us and sent "prana" rays of communication into the space and to each other. Stanislavski said "send the prana there – I want to reach through the tip of my finger – to God – the sky – or, later on, my partner. I believe my inner energy and I give it out – I spread it."'[41] Soloviova's recollection tallies with exercises Stanislavsky gave to opera singers from the Bolshoi Opera with whom he worked between 1921 and 1926. Once again, he focuses on letting '*prana* energy flow to the end of your outstretched hand, releasing all tension right down to the tips of your fingers. Remember: the fingers are all important.' He makes a direct correlation between the flow of energy and the fluency of a student's movement, noting that dancing or gymnastics 'cannot give you this plasticity as long as you do not possess an inner sense of movement. When you walk your energy must flow all the way from your spine down your legs. This is something you should be stubborn about acquiring. Only then will your body be flexible.'[42] Stanislavsky's claims for yoga are interesting in that they bring together several aspects of an actor's work from plasticity to the attentional state of relaxed concentration, both of which enhance their quality of communication or projection.

---

[38]Stanislavsky 2008b: 246.
[39]Stanislavski 1980: 199.
[40]Gordon 1987: 31.
[41]In Zarrilli 2009: 14.
[42]Stanislavsky and Rumantsev 1998: 327.